The Eye of the Master

CARLETON LIBRARY SERIES

The Carleton Library Series publishes books about Canadian economics, geography, history, politics, public policy, society and culture, and related topics, in the form of leading new scholarship and reprints of classics in these fields. The series is funded by Carleton University, published by McGill-Queen's University Press, and is under the guidance of the Carleton Library Series Editorial Board, which consists of faculty members of Carleton University. Suggestions and proposals for manuscripts and new editions of classic works are welcome and may be directed to the Carleton Library Series Editorial Board c/o the Library, Carleton University, Ottawa K1S 5B6, at cls@carleton.ca, or on the web at www.carleton.ca/cls.

The Eye of the Master

Figures of the Québécois Colonial Imaginary

DALIE GIROUX

Translated by Jennifer Henderson

Carleton Library Series 262

McGill-Queen's University Press
Montreal & Kingston • London • Chicago

© McGill-Queen's University Press 2023
Originally published in French as *L'oeil du maître* ©2020 Mémoire d'encrier

ISBN 978-0-2280-1637-3 cloth
ISBN 978-0-2280-1638-0 ePDF
ISBN 978-0-2280-1639-7 ePUB

Legal deposit second quarter of 2023

Printed in Canada on acid-free paper that is 100% ancient forest free (100% post-consumer recycled), processed chlorine free

This book has been published with the help of a grant from the Canadian Federation for the Humanities and Social Sciences, through the Awards to Scholarly Publications Program, using funds provided by the Social Sciences and Humanities Research Council of Canada.

Funded by the Government of Canada · Financé par le gouvernement du Canada | Canadä · Canada Council for the Arts · Conseil des arts du Canada

We acknowledge the support of the Canada Council for the Arts.
Nous remercions le Conseil des arts du Canada de son soutien.

Library and Archives Canada Cataloguing in Publication

Title: The eye of the master : figures of the Québécois colonial imaginary / Dalie Giroux ; translated by Jennifer Henderson.
Other titles: L'oeil du maître. English
Names: Giroux, Dalie, 1974- author. | Henderson, Jennifer (Jennifer Anne), translator.
Series: Carleton library series ; 262.
Description: Series statement: Carleton Library series ; 262 | Originally published in French as L'oeil du maître. | Includes bibliographical references.
Identifiers: Canadiana (print) 20220450684 | Canadiana (ebook) 20220450730 | ISBN 9780228016373 (cloth) | ISBN 9780228016397 (ePUB) | ISBN 9780228016380 (ePDF)
Subjects: LCSH: Nationalism—Québec (Province) | LCSH: Decolonization—Social aspects—Québec (Province) | LCSH: Québec (Province)—History—Autonomy and independence movements. | CSH: Quebeckers—Ethnic identity.
Classification: LCC FC2920.S6 G5713 2023 | DDC 320.1/509714—dc23

Contents

Figures

For a Decolonization from Below: Translator's Introduction to *The Eye of the Master*

JENNIFER HENDERSON

"The Eye of the Master" is an old fable retold by Jean de La Fontaine. For Dalie Giroux, the fable speaks of a sacrificial organization of power, a way of seeing and relating that sustains exploitation, exclusion, and the violent interruption of nascent solidarities. Fables are not pieces of rarefied culture; they belong to the realm of the popular, and so, for Giroux, the zone of reference of this ancient fable overlaps with everyday cultural materials like the highway sign – seen on Autoroute 640, north of Montreal: "Boulevard des Entreprises," "Boulevard des Seigneurs" – or the political slogan, "masters in our own house," a phrase identified with sovereigntist aspirations in Quebec since the late 1960s. La Fontaine's fable seems to crystallize the ethos of that political rallying cry, offering admiration for the power of the master's eye and under-lining the necessity of the sacrificial order which that eye oversees.

The fable itself seems quite simple. A stag takes refuge in a stable of oxen, promising to show the oxen the best parts of the commons outside if they will just hide him for a while. Servants come and go; no one observes the stag; the oxen keep his presence a secret. Then the master arrives to do his rounds. His sharp eye locates the trembling stranger amidst his stock. Immediately, everyone descends on the stag, who is butchered and served up in a joyous feast, to which all the neighbours are invited.

The fable is related by La Fontaine's storyteller without explicit judgement or point of view until the end, when two lines are quoted from an earlier teller, Phaedrus, the freed Roman slave who was the first to transcribe Aesop's fables: "The master's eye the best surveys. / But I prefer the lover's piercing gaze."[1]

If not exactly an interpretation, the lines offer a sudden detachment, the possibility of seeing otherwise. Opposing the lover's eye to the master's, they suggest that the lover's way of seeing is preferable, or equally powerful. The concluding lines have a destabilizing effect; suddenly, ambiguities proliferate.

The oxen do not know the world outside the stable; the stag has much to teach them. On the other hand, within the stable, they have a master who sees to their care. Does he not rage at the servants who allow their mangers to become empty of grass and their yokes to lie in careless disarray? At the same time, what is the nature of the care and security offered by the stable? What is this order that the stag enters? The oxen protect the stag; on the other hand, the fable does not tell us anything about the oxen as witnesses. When the stag is spotted by the master, do the oxen observe complacently, or hopelessly, or spitefully? What does it mean to them that their stable could never be a safe place for the stag? When we are told that "Each fell upon him with his long boar-spear,"[2] the "each" who collaborate spontaneously in the violence, once the stag is exposed, probably refers to the servants. But why do the servants themselves not see the stag before this point? Do they only pretend not to? Are they, too, subject to the master's eye? The all-seeing master is fearsome; however, he generously shares out the meat at the end. What is the nature of this neighbourly distribution, this "public good"? Should we approve of the order of the stable, or should we think of its terrible cost? And for whom? For the stag alone, or also for the oxen, and maybe even the servants? It is through the lover's eye, invoked through the reference to Phaedrus at the end, that these ambiguities become apparent. It turns out that the fable, while appearing to stress the singular sharpness of the master's eye, is also about the potential counter-force of the lover's eye, which is perhaps the same as the sharp reader's eye,[3] or indeed – to shift away from visual primacy – the discernment of the good listener.

This is what the twentieth-century Québécois rallying cry, "masters in our own house," misses, inasmuch as it circulates a unidimensional version of La Fontaine's slyly ambiguous fable, overlooking its warning about the master's eye. The master's eye "has better insight than anyone else when it comes to his own business,"[4] but the master's business is not the only possible version of the world. There is no necessity to the order of the stable; there are questions to ask, questions that point to other possible ways of living and relating. This opening onto instability is what Giroux's *The Eye of the Master* pursues, as it asks how the order of the stable came to be so widely projected and so deeply normalized in Quebec, indeed in settler-colonial North America more generally insofar as it is bent on productivity and accumulation. The allegorical interpretation of the fable in terms of settler-colonial relations is quite evident: the stag's experience tells of the capture, sacrifice, and sharing out of the Indigenous, for a "public" benefit. But the fable also introduces nuance and complexity to the settler/Indigenous binary: the order of the stable is maintained from different positions and in different ways, by the master, the servants, and perhaps the oxen themselves, even though this order reduces their existence. It is the multivalent, collective investment in the master's eye that this book aims to unsettle. Giroux does not offer a closed interpretation and indeed nudges the reader to see that the stag also could be the refugee or the hijab-wearing woman in present-day Quebec. The emphasis could be placed on the insecure sanctuary of the stable, or at the level of its ambiguous and shifting identifications, the fable's uncomfortable slide from fear for the stag to happy community feast. Equally, emphasis could be placed on the nascent, brutally disrupted solidarity of oxen and stag, and what the stag had to teach.

Like La Fontaine's fable of the same name, Giroux's *The Eye of the Master* describes a political and socio-economic order and gestures at an alternative one. In the penultimate chapter, Giroux invites readers to notice that the master's eye, that organ of capture and control, is "quivering," and "dissonant sounds" can be heard. The shift from the eye to the ear suggests another mode of theorizing, one that seeks to remove itself from theory as an enterprise connected to the social power of the master's eye. "Theory" is from the Latin *theoria,* meaning "vision, [a] branch of study that deals with contemplation, speculation, or the theoretical approach as opposed to the practical" (OED). Giroux's political theorizing neither proceeds from a remote and comfortable distance, nor claims a master's total and final seeing. In proposing the shift from eye to ear (and other senses) as its figure for the renewal of critical practice, *The Eye of the Master* resonates with a strand of queer theorizing of sociality in the Anglo-American world which focuses on "an elsewhere that is first perceptible as atmosphere," something disrupted and "refunctioned" in "aural mediation," perhaps in a barely discernable "glitch."[5] But while this remarkable book shares queer theory's project of "detachment from the normal,"[6] the book's engagement with the intimate, with affect, is, in the first

instance, about *colonial* normalcy – and more precisely the specific vernaculars, slogans, myths, highway signage, sound-image complexes, family photographs, rural *habitus*, and ordinary racisms that express the history and
present of a Quebec which has sought to attain mastery in its own house
through colonial conquest. *The Eye of the Master* incites ongoing interpretation of La Fontaine's fable, its application and reapplication to the social world
in such a way as to recognize the numerous dynamics it might speak of, the
complex social relations and seemingly permanent structures of power that
can be read through it.

• • •

Dalie Giroux is a political theorist who cares for semi-retired hens. Between
the eight of them, the *filles* produce at most an egg a day. There is a whole
ethos of care and relation, beyond – and indeed, radically other to – the master's tending to his oxen, in the sustaining of this little free-ranging post-work
commune. Materialist feminists might see in it a commitment to reciprocating
the labour of care, or social reproduction. Anti-capitalist anarchists might see
a refusal of the order of the stable, with its bargain of disciplined productivity
exchanged for the security of captivity. Readers of *The Eye of the Master* will
most certainly recognize in it the enactment of an understanding of responsibility and relationality which Giroux's portrait of herself as an assiduous
reader of Indigenous philosophy tells us comes, in a very significant part, from
a humble and deliberate project of unlearning colonial entitlement – an ongoing project, which always takes place in situ.[7]

Giroux was born in the 1970s across the river from Quebec City, in the blue-
collar town of Lévis. The Giroux and Laflamme families did not go to university but Giroux had access to the rich library left behind by an aunt who,
having immersed herself in the 1960s French and Québécois literature and
philosophy of cultural and political change, had taken off for Vancouver, never
to return.[8] At the age of twelve, Giroux took up residence in the aunt's room
in her grandmother's house, and so, surrounded by the "René Lévesque relics"
on the walls of this working-class house, and while attending a secondary
school at which she was taught by the Grey Nuns, she embarked on a first,
adolescent journey into the consciousness of difference. Attending CÉGEP in
the period of the failed Charlottetown Accord, Giroux was a youthful reader

of *Le Devoir*'s coverage of debates over constitutional reform, which would have packaged together the liberal recognitions of Quebec as a "distinct society," of Indigenous self-government in limited forms, and – importantly for Giroux's later thinking about resource development on the unceded Indigenous territories of Anishinabewaki, Eeyou Istchee, and Nitassinan – provincial jurisdiction over forestry, mining, and regional development. Studying politics at Laval University and then the Université du Québec à Montréal, Giroux would be profoundly influenced by the work of Michel Foucault, Gilles Deleuze, and Félix Guattari, while reading Kafka, among others, in her spare time.[9] In her youth, she also benefitted from the informal pedagogy of another aunt, who provided an initiation into countercultural ways of life. Giroux's sense of indebtedness to these two aunts suggests one more source, and one more frame of reference, for the praxis of caring, with a sense of pleasure and wonder, for unruly retired hens.[10]

Giroux writes, in part, from a childhood experience of poverty, but also from a schooling in diverse critiques of capitalism which has produced an approach that is nomadic and non-doctrinaire, open to exploration of the unconscious, the effects of power/knowledge, the critique of morals, transculturalism, the flâneur's art of collecting debris and ruin, and a certain pleasure in the absurd. She is a political philosopher whose interdisciplinary introduction to political studies through Carol Levasseur[11] at Laval defied the boundaries of politics as "science" and whose doctorate at UQAM coincided with an opening, in that context, to methodological originality and creative eccentricity.[12] Giroux's early collaboration with members of the Groupe de recherche sur les imaginaires politiques en Amérique latine (GRIPAL) has expanded into wide and varied collaborative practice in both academic and artistic contexts.[13] A number of collaborations have consisted in efforts to bring the work of decolonial scholars in Quebec to wider audiences (*Robert Hébert: La réception impossible*, edited with Simon Labrecque; Jean Morisset's *Sur la piste du Canada errant*, which Giroux helped to edit; and Wendat philosopher and Giroux's University of Ottawa colleague Georges E. Sioui's *Histoires de Kanatha: Vues et contées/Histories of Kanatha: Seen and Told*, which she selected and introduced). Giroux translated the work of the Mohawk sociologist Patricia Monture for the journal *Recherches féministes*. She was co-founder, with Sébastien Mussi, of the scholarly journal *Les Cahiers de l'idiotie*, whose fifth issue, devoted to the topic "Merde," or "shit," she edited. She contributes regularly to a number of Quebec journals of ideas: from militant publications such as *À bâbord!*, *Nouveaux cahiers du socialisme*, and *Relations*, to journals for the discussion of art and culture, such as *Spirale* and *Liberté*.

L'œil du maître – The Eye of the Master – was released in the fall of 2020 by Mémoire d'encrier, an independent Montreal-based publisher founded in 2003 by the Haitian-Québécois poet, editor, and translator Rodney Saint-Éloi, with a commitment to fostering a transcultural Québécois space of diversity and foregrounding of global and Indigenous literatures.[14] For francophone Québécois readers of cultural and political commentary, the name Dalie Giroux was already associated with provocative writing that renewed the genre of the polemical essay in a distinctively poetic and sometimes caustic style, and rejected a nationalist master narrative of Quebec identity. Giroux's third book in four years, *L'œil du maître* extends themes and approaches that are distinctively Girouxian: dispossession in colonial North America, the phenomenology of life captured by state and capital, an unsparing exploration of vernacular Québécois culture, or what one nationalist critic of Giroux's 2017 collection, *Le Québec brûle en enfer*, describes with distaste as an interest in the "ugly and the strange in collective life."[15] What is different about *L'œil du maître* is that it turns very specifically to the dissection of settler colonialism in modern Quebec. It is a slim volume of sharp "incisions into the rhetoric of 'masters in our own house.'"[16]

...

As implied in the book's subtitle, *Figures de l'imaginaire colonial Québécois*, Giroux accounts for the interminable life of the slogan "masters in our own house" by turning to the collective imaginary. She identifies tropes that work to bind feelings of shame, nostalgia, rancour, and especially envy into a Québécois "psychopolitics" bent on taking the place of the master-proprietor. The fantasy of "the people as Boss" runs through everyday racist practices and colonial performativities, from encircling hijab-wearing women to playing "cowboys and Indians"; it is in the family photo album as well as on the political stage. It is exemplified in the refusals by sovereigntists to respond to Indigenous invitations to alliance in the latter half of the 1970s, in a spectacular failure to envision a continental decolonialism. These refusals, grounded in a unidimensional analysis of colonial power as federal power and a jealous possessiveness of the position of victim, are recounted by Giroux in painful detail.[17] When it comes to an ethics of decolonization, a willingness to meet the Cree, the Innu, the Algonquin-Anishinaabeg and the Atikamekw nations on an equal footing, there is little to distinguish the social democratic Parti Québécois of the 1970s from the party of the right, Coalition Avenir Québec, in government in Quebec since 2018. Giroux makes this argument as a person who, with family and friends in her youth, as she tells us, mourned the defeat of the "yes" vote for sovereignty in the 1980 and 1995 referenda. She draws a distinction between the nationalist and colonial project of sovereignty and the broader one of *indépendance*, which still might be turned to a more complex analysis of power and the humility necessary to finding a place within a "chain of solidarity" that would link the struggles for life outside the master's stable.

The question *L'œil du maître* asks, then, is what, in the shared imaginary of white, francophone Québécois seeing themselves as descending from seventeenth- and eighteenth-century New France, accounts for the consistent preference for colonialism over emancipation? What can explain the preference for some future mastery over a fenced house instead of participation in alliances which already, in certain pockets of the here and now, prefigure an equitable, radically hospitable alternative? In order to contribute to answering this question, Giroux acts as a *bricoleur*, combining the tools of historiography, auto-ethnography, a structuralist analysis of myth, and the materialist critic's constellation of disparate cultural materials. This practice of juxtaposing what only seems disparate, especially in terms of linear time and the opposition of the "modern" to the "outmoded," was modelled by the German Jewish critic Walter Benjamin, as a way of jamming the illusion of progress. Giroux also constellates the intimate and familial with the public and political, the mundane with the extraordinary and spectacular. Her surprising juxtapositions contest the specific progress narrative according to which the exploitation of human and natural resources, and the fetishization of productivity, eventually bring wealth for all, with assimilation as a side benefit. It is not just that this narrative blocks solidarities and necessitates the repeated sacrifice of the stag, it also pretends that the ethos of the stable constantly improves on the past. Against that view, Giroux stresses historical missed opportunities for decolonial alliance, passageways not taken (and indeed barred off), and voices ignored or submerged in the decades of Québécois state-building through resource extraction on unceded lands, from the hydro-electrical damming of La Grande River in James Bay in the 1970s to the mining and LNG projects on the Côte-Nord in the present.

Giroux's point is that the opportunity for intersectional solidarity is not new. Throughout *L'œil du maître* – and in spite of the book's interest in the power of a governing myth and its diagnosis of a deep psychopolitical block-age – the political argument stresses contingency and accident, plural possi-bilities, and the fact that there was nothing of necessity or destiny in the route taken by modern Quebec. Giroux draws on the work of the late anthropolo-gist Rémi Savard, a member of the Laboratoire d'anthropologie amérindi-enne de Montréal, who, early on and repeatedly, denounced the failure to align *indépendance* with Indigenous struggle and anti-racism. But most piv-otal to the *detournement* that this book brings about with regard to the nor-malized pursuit of mastery is Giroux's engagement with the philosophy, autobiography, and oral traditions of Innu and Wendat writers. Passages from the 1976 autobiography of the Innu writer, activist, and knowledge keeper An Antane Kapesh puncture the "colonial façade" of Indigenous primitivism and European ingenuity.[18] The Wendat philosopher Georges E. Sioui, provides the theory of accidental European colonialism – based on flight from sickness and opportunism – as well as the model of radically open hospitality. For Giroux, the key to dismantling the sacrificial order of maximally productive livestock and stags quickly rounded up for slaughter is the centring of local Indigenous thought and struggle. She writes, "it will be impossible to unsettle the structures of exclusion that reproduce xenophobia, racism, and anti-im-migration politics unless we place Indigenous issues at the heart of political life in Quebec."

L'œil du maître has been warmly received by francophone Québécois re-viewers and prize committees. The book was reviewed in the major French-language newspapers and in numerous journals of contemporary culture and political commentary, sometimes in pieces accompanied by interviews with the author. It has won two prestigious prizes, the 2021 Quebec Academy of Letters' Victor-Barbeau Prize and the 2020–21 Spirale Eva-Le-Grand Prize; it was also a jury selection for both the 2021 Grand Prix du livre de Montréal and the 2022 Prix des libraires du Québec. The book's reception may speak of a generation of Québécois readers ready to discard the conventional defenses against reckoning with settler colonialism and systemic racism, and already making the connections – between Indigenous knowledge, climate justice, and refugee rights, between large-scale resource extraction and the undead spirit of the buccaneer – which *L'œil du maître* draws so persuasively. A columnist in *La Presse* identified with Giroux as a Québécoise of her own generation, raised "within the dream of sovereignty" but disenchanted with its identitarianism.[19] The generational explanation for the book's laudatory reception may be insufficient, however.

There has long been more room in Quebec than in English Canada for the publication of the philosophical and political essay outside the system of university presses; the longstanding place for reflective, engaged writing, lighter on scholarly apparatus and more poetic than "scientific," on the lists of independent publishers in Quebec is part of a context that nourishes interventions such as *L'œil du maître*. Québécois print culture also has undergone a period of renewal in the past decade, with the appearance of new publishers, journals, and networks of writers.[20] The growing prominence of a publishing house such as Mémoire d'encrier speaks of a diversification in access to the means of producing and disseminating discourse in Quebec, at least in Montreal. A piece in *La Presse* in 2021 called attention to the emergence of the literature of a "new left" in Quebec and, in a list of readings representing this wave of repoliticization and its mark on publishing, placed *L'œil du maître* alongside, among others, Rosa Pire's *Ne sommes-nous pas Québécoises?*, on second-generation immigrant women's experiences of racism in Quebec; *Kuei, je te salue: Conversation sur le racisme*, an epistolary exchange between the Innu poet Natasha Kanapé Fontaine and the Québécois-American novelist Deni Ellis Béchard; and *NoirEs sous surveillance: Esclavage, répression, violence d'État au Canada*, the translation of Robyn Maynard's *Policing Black Lives*.[21] One might add to this list the novels of the Innu writer Naomi Fontaine and the work of the Essipiunnu sociologist and poet Pierrot Ross-Tremblay. Academic publishing has also seen a wave of studies introducing settler-colonial theory to Québécois historiography (Sean Mills, Catherine Larochelle, David Meren, Daniel Rück) and cultural studies (Julie Burelle, Bruno Cornellier, Caroline Desbiens).

Giroux's call for a polyvocal alliance against the "civilization of expropriation, extraction, accumulation, and destruction," for a wholesale questioning

of the concepts of nation and property, which she sees as leading to the constant renewal of colonialism, has been criticized, by several otherwise sym-
pathetic francophone reviewers, as too idealist, offering "poetic metaphors"
instead of "concrete and realistic" proposals.[22] The book's title, though, is a
reminder of the political potency of metaphor, and Giroux's intervention is
precisely at the level of the political imagination. She does not just diagnose
ethical and epistemological blockages in stubbornly persistent tropes, she also
proposes alternative figures she sees as capable of sustaining another kind of
imaginary. These figures speak of place, history, and possibility. "Roxham
Road" is one: Giroux marshalls the place-name, which many readers will recognize as the historically uncontrolled border crossing near the junction of
Quebec Autoroute 15 and Interstate Highway 87 in New York that has been
an irregular entry point for asylum seekers arriving in Quebec via the US since
2017, as a metonym for finding "passageways within barriers" and the possibility of a wider practice of Georges E. Sioui's ethos of radical hospitality.

   Another alternative trope is offered near the end of the book, in an image
which stands for four hundred years of missed opportunities for decolonial
alliance. Giroux invites readers to return imaginatively to "Sainte-Barbe," an
archaic naval expression for the part of the transatlantic vessel in which the
poorer class of passenger, the indentured workers and immigrants without
means, slept.[23] She means to underline a positioning and an experience that
was not the same as that of the dehumanized cargo in the ship's hold – one
that was ambiguous in class terms, and needs to be understood historically.
Giroux asks, what if those "hired men of New France," below deck on those
ships also transporting enslaved Africans, had been capable of recognizing
and respecting their fellow humans, chained below them in the hold; and
more than that, what if they had been capable of seizing the conditions ripe
for a multitudinous revolt? Importantly, this thought experiment is meant to
stress continguity, and the unrealized possibility of solidarity, rather than
comparable positionings. As Giroux has written elsewhere, with reference to
the infamous appropriation and metaphorization of chattel slavery to signify
the status of French Canadians by the 1960s *felquiste* Pierre Vallières:[24] "To
call the exploited labourer a slave is not a very good metaphor. And it is ultimately disrespectful to the history of slavery, to those who remember this
history. It's not the same thing to arrive, enchained within a stall on a boat,
to be sold as merchandise, after having been kidnapped from another conti-

nent, as it is to sign a three-year bonding contract as a dispossessed worker, in which you still retain the rights to your own person."[25] In her insistence on a continental, even hemispheric geography of colonialism and the "arc between Quebec and the Caribbean evok[ing] the commerce around the Atlantic," Giroux is clear: those "hired men of New France," when they became the celebrated *coureurs de bois* and *voyageurs* of the fur trade, entered history as the cousins of the plundering buccaneers to the south. But it did not have to be so.

Giroux addresses Vallières only briefly in *L'œil du maître*. She observes that he became a vocal supporter of the assertion of Indigenous sovereignty, in the decade following his 1968 anti-colonial salvo. (In an earlier publication, Giroux discusses the Longeuil "shantytown"-raised Vallières as the bearer of a "gangrene of infinite humiliation," which manifested itself in his misogynist understanding of his mother, in addition to the racist metaphor.[26] Giroux is a resolutely intersectional thinker.) In *L'œil du maître*, it is through the figure of the *mauvais pauvre* that Giroux engages with the longer history of attempts to name the specific politico-economic subjection and socio-psychic[27] abjection of working-class white French Canadians. The plural form, *mauvais pauvres*, translated here as "the paupers of settler colonialism,"[28] is a phrase that bears something of the terms *lumpenproletariat*, the undeserving poor, and "white trash"; however, none of these expressions contains the psychic dimension of self-loathing which is important to its original usage by Hector Saint-Denys Garneau, the poet of the 1950s, as well as to subsequent interpretations, including Giroux's.[29] In *L'œil du maître*, the figure implicitly replaces Vallières' ill-considered metaphor and also insists on a more deeply ambivalent subject position for white, working-class Québécois: the *mauvais pauvre* is part denigrated, humiliated, abused and exploited (in Giroux's words, one of "the guys I went to school with, in the county of Bellechasse, taking fentanyl in their decrepit family homes by the manure-poisoned fields bordering highway 132, waiting for the apocalyptic miracle of the third link"[30]), and part twenty-first-century buccaneer, a pathetic show-off. Neither does the *mauvais pauvre* serve as a wholly adequate figure. In Giroux's text, the figure is not the last word, not the final, authoritative "correction" of Vallières' appropriative metaphor. In the course of the discussion in chapter 5, *mauvais pauvre* slides into a new figure, the "Keb," an apocope which Giroux borrows from urban discourse: it is a term used to redescribe those who refer to themselves as Québécois *de souche*, or

FOR A DECOLONIZATION FROM BELOW

old-stock Québécois, from a slant, sometimes disdainful, but certainly wry and knowing perspective.

Highlighting the operations of difference and deferral in naming is a gesture well suited to a book that questions the need for mastery. Together, the chapters of *L'œil du maître* are intended to be an *essai*, in the sense of an exploration, and also in the more specific sense of the intellectual essay as a genre: theoretical and poetic, self-reflective, fragmented, incomplete, an "experiment in attention."[31] In its nomination for the Victor-Barbeau Prize, which recognizes contributions to the genre of the essay, the book was cited for its remarkable stylistic hybridity: Giroux was praised for "not hesitating to use the "I," to plunge into family archives, to alternate between passages in an academic tone and freer passages which are lyrical, explosive, even punk."[32] One of the most striking elements of Giroux's essayistic style is her inclusion of the enunciating subject, the writing "I," in its interaction with the world. In chapter 4, this element becomes the basis for an examination of the material embeddedness of Giroux's own family in a kind of everyday colonial structure of feeling. Her grandfather, she tells us, repaired the radios and television sets through which a white Québécois world, with Indigenous presence evacuated or rendered as the primitive past, was disseminated. This is neither confession nor abstract sociology, but rather part of a textured, auto-ethnographic tracing of the interweaving of settler-colonial affect and class *habitus*. For the anglophone field of settler-colonial studies, dominated by the methods and discourses of the social sciences, *L'œil du maître* provides a valuable demonstration of more experimental and hybrid approaches, interested in such messy particularity.

What Giroux stresses in the *mauvais pauvre* is the sense of having nothing and being nothing, which can fuel dangerous sentiments of envy and defensive colonial nostalgia. She positions herself as the inheritor of this envy, of which she was acutely aware in the early days of her friendship with the Wendat philosopher Georges E. Sioui, when she shared with him her mourned lack of a "heritage that would constitute a *codex* of liberty in this territory," her feeling that "the inheritance I have, I do not want." Giroux includes this moment of encounter as part of the story of her own education, as a Québécoise political theorist, through engagement with the writing of the Indigenous renaissance. A list of Indigenous writers, from the Métis activist Howard Adams, to the Sto:lo novelist Lee Maracle, is Giroux's inventory of her decolonial influences, her acknowledgement of the conditions of possibility for her intellectual formation. One Québécois critic has found the auto-ethnographic element of *L'œil du maître* to skirt uncomfortably closely to self-flagellation.[33] The charge raises the question of why this self-exposure, offering one possible model of the difficult work to be done on a wider scale in Quebec, should have garnered so many prizes and awards, if it cuts so close to the bone. The question should be of particular interest to anglophone Canadian readers, who will encounter this English translation in the context of a very long self-congratulatory tradition, among Canadian commentators, of claiming a comparative progressivism for Canada. They should take care not to read the urgency of Giroux's call for critical reflexivity as evidence of Quebec's lagging in comparison to Canada's readiness for decolonization. Historically, such a sense of moral superiority has been aligned with an imperial posture. French Canadians were described as "destitute of all that can invigorate and elevate a people" in the 1839 *Report of Lord Durham on the Affairs of British North America*.[34] That diagnosis of moral backwardness, by an English liberal reformer, came with a recommendation to establish the "national character" of the British Empire in the rebellious colony then called Lower Canada, in order to give the otherwise "stationary" francophone Catholics the chance at becoming something other than "labourers in the employ of English capitalists."[35] Assimilation would be the key to greater equality, in this liberal-capitalist vision. Clearly, this is not Giroux's vision. She keeps readers aware of this angle of the master's eye through linguistic and typographical techniques of distanciation, writing "the Province of Quebec" and "*british-canadian*" in the midst of her French prose, to keep the living traces of that particular empire in view. The effect is of course diminished in an English translation, but more challenging still is the presentation of a genealogy of a certain kind of Québécois abjection, colonial and racist in its political and cultural expression, to an anglophone readership.

Unavoidably, an English translation enters a field of Canadian nationalist discourse marked by "competitive manipulations" in which the "multicultural mosaic" – and we might add, flattened versions of "reconciliation" – are marshalled as "ideological sleight[s] of hand pitted against Quebec's presumably greater cultural homogeneity."[36] Currently, Quebec's Act respecting the laicity of the State, passed as Bill 21 in 2019,[37] is generating opposition both within and outside of Quebec, with stands taken by a number of municipalities in the "rest of Canada," offering to support legal challenges to the discriminatory law.[38] There has been less publicity regarding the failure on the part of all three federal parties to address the multi-pronged recommendations issued by the 2021 National Summit on Islamophobia, which discuss Quebec's Bill 21 alongside Canada Border Services' targeting of Muslim refugees and the Canada Revenue Agency's systemic bias in the auditing and revocation of Muslim charities, among other things.[39] At the end of the day, this is a game between colonial-capitalist nation-statisms, in which the unspoken stake is control over the narrative that can make sense of white supremacy, exclusion, and exploitation. With that narrative in mind, anglophone readers will decide for themselves whom this book is for; its vision of solidarity and friendship is capacious, though uncompromising. Giroux's genealogy of Québécois settler colonialism offers the tools of a deeply nuanced, intersectional analysis and a method of exploratory self-examination, attuned to what vernaculars can reveal about the *dispositifs* of dispossession we are stuck inside and involved in reproducing. And not just in Quebec.

Within the contemporary politics of recognition in Canada, the appropriative claiming of Indigenous identity is a manoeuvre through which some have been attempting to reassert control, in Quebec as in Canada.[40] Giroux criticizes those who adopt the cloak of *métissage* in Quebec but her energy is focused on developing a different kind of intervention into the historical self-understanding that could produce the aggressive posture of Quebec's recent Bill 21 and, decades before that legislation, the modern colonial project of conquering unceded Indigenous lands within provincial boundaries in the name of Québécois sovereignty. Giroux's political instincts are non-identitarian. Wary of denunciatory dynamics, she is more interested in what she calls the "psychic, intimate matter of colonialism," in other words, the murky, the unconscious, the contradictory and ambivalent, the wounds, the defenses, the delusions. She wants to know how the potential for solidarity was ruined, and she synthesizes critiques of capital and the state-form in order to show how the tactics of enclosing populations and declaring a right of pre-emption[41] created the conditions for contemporary racisms and ongoing colonial predations. The appropriation of Indigenous identity in order to diffuse and confuse the grounds for struggle is one of the current expressions of those colonial-capitalist relations.

Under the heading "Revisiting the Ethnogenesis of Québécois Nationalism" in chapter 1, Giroux proposes a reading of history "from below," according to which the claim to a sovereign right inherited from the French elites involved in the establishment of New France is a spurious, backwards projection of twentieth-century colonial ambitions. This illegitimate claim covers over, in a discourse of restored continuity if not destiny, the moment of decision, the element of contingency, in the history of those who eventually made themselves into the Québécois. Among the motley subalterns who were transported from France to the banks of the Saint Lawrence River in the seventeenth century, there was no uniform identification with the French Crown; neither, among this "formless, disorderly laboring class," the "hewers of wood and drawers of water," as they have been called elsewhere,[42] was there a uniform legal entitlement to possession of the soil. The distribution of that entitlement was a later, twentieth-century project, one which had to channel the distrust of institutionalized power, inherited from generations of French Canadians who had experienced the sharp end of the collaboration of Church and capital to ensure their subservience, into the demand for a piece of the colonial pie.

Giroux argues that there is no colonial right, no "French colonial prerogative," inherited by the Québécois. The "archaic segment" of the population – a "bastard" people, too motley to constitute any kind of coherent origin – passed from French rulers to British ones; then, in the last third of the twentieth century, its rulers won some of the trappings of *"british-canadian"* colonial power for themselves. Giroux stresses discontinuity and class hierarchy: a "little nineteenth-century entrepreneurial elite" became a "clerical one draping itself in a 'French' aura in the early twentieth century, and then a bureaucratic and cultural one beginning in the 1960s." The argument is an attempt to undermine identification with the agrarian myth of the contented *habitant* and the sense of entitlement that identification seems to sustain in the present. Giroux uses the technique of the list to redescribe the "archaic segment" as transported subalterns who were white, but illiterate, and available for *"de facto* transfer" from one European regime to another precisely because of their insecure positioning within relations of production. Her inventories of this formless class, made up of people in states of relative dispossession, suggest the inadequacy of existing analytical categories, since as a form for gathering, the list is always frustrated by variety and incompletion.[43]

Readers will recognize another strategy for undermining entitlement in Giroux's ironic use of the phrase "populations required for settlement" as something of a refrain. She borrows (a version of) the phrase from the legal reasoning in the 1997 *Delgamuukw v. British Columbia* decision, which, among other things, spelled out the conditions which, in the eyes of the law, justified infringement of aboriginal title, including "the building of infrastructure and the settlement of foreign populations to support those aims."[44] It is difficult to ground a claim to colonial right in this history of serving as the pawns of empire. Of course, there is the risk that this alternative story of a residual, illiterate population might be taken up as a way of dodging accountability for implication in settler-colonial relations in the present. But Giroux is clear that today, the Québécois control a settler-colonial state that claims legal prerogative and undertakes massive colonial endeavours. She places her bet on the possibilities of subversive, "heretical" friendship and creative, local alliances. This is an account of a missed opportunity for allied revolt among the variously dispossessed, in the name of a whole other mode of relation among beings, and to the planet, grounded in Indigenous knowledge and governance. Thus, its acknowledgement of a subaltern, "bastard" (non-)origin comes with a strong warning against the kind of unidimensional identification with victimhood that only serves to launch a compensatory pursuit of mastery. The history of settler colonialism in modern Quebec provides that warning. And so, says Giroux, *Il faut nuancer*.

• • •

In order to preserve a trace of Giroux's penchant for defamiliarization, I have retained the French-language use of the lowercase for "british-canadian," which Giroux italicizes to mark its foreignness in the midst of her prose. French names for groups or places are not translated when these are well-known to English speakers in Canada. While those decisions have been made with a view to preserving, rather than erasing, the traces of translation, the translator's notes in this edition are added in hopes that readers without extensive knowledge of Quebec and Canadian politics and history will not miss out on the richness of this text.

• • •

I wish to thank Dalie Giroux for her generous responses to my questions and Peter Hodgins and Jody Mason for their valuable feedback on a draft of this introduction. Additional thanks to Correy Baldwin for his meticulous copy-editing.

The Eye of the Master

Introduction:
Masters in Our Own House?

"Masters in our own house" is a proverbial phrase in the Saint Lawrence River valley. Beyond party differences, the phrase condenses dominant Québécois political thought of the second half of the twentieth century. It is a call to action, driving a collective aspiration to a quiet revolution that would dismantle the economic, political, legal, and cultural subjugation of French Canadians resulting from the Franco-British imperial adventure in America. The slogan was first sounded in 1962, in the context of a historic provincial electoral campaign,[1] on the basis of which the Quebec state would spearhead a strategy of natural resource control and social and economic development for its majority francophone population. Quebec would enter modernity, the promise went, and French Canadians would become a collective political subject, finally seizing the means of their self-determination.

The slogan, "Masters in our own house," is the political and intellectual inheritance of my generation, as is the sovereigntist project of Quebec in the 1960s and 1970s which followed logically from it. I was born in 1974; I saw the light of day in a public hospital; my father raised his family on the basis of a salary earned in the great James Bay construction sites; I was educated in free state schools from kindergarten to PhD; and I was a first-hand witness of the two "lost" referenda on the question of Quebec sovereignty, in 1980 and 1995. My parents were born French Canadian. For my part, I was born Québécois just as the political fervor that nourished the liberation movement reached its peak and just as modernity, Quebec-style, came to fruition.

"Masters in our own house" evokes at once a national territory – the "own house" – and a triumphant passage from a state of servitude to a state of mastery. It is immediately clear that political freedom is being framed in specifically national and ethnic terms. The narrative implied in the phrase has a particular collective subject, with its own traits, complicities, and hatreds: it is Leviathan on the franco-northern colonial scene. Indeed, the Quiet Revolution² and the sovereigntist project would come to name and, to some extent, realize a liberation that was specifically for the descendants of the old French Canada, of which I am one (although without benefit of the masculine prestige associated with that heritage). The identitarian turn of Québécois nationalism in the last two decades is a return to this ethnic impulse, rather than a deviation from it.

Emilie Nicolas, in a recent essay, underlines the ambivalence of the Québécois phrase, "masters in our own house," as well as the fundamental stumbling block in the racial distinction it implicitly asserts:

> When we said *white n—*,³ did we aspire to abolish racial inequalities or rather to take up a position based on the "rights" of the inheritors of French civilization? Did we seek to end economic exploitation or to become the "Boss" as a people? Having deployed *white n—* as a figure for our own struggle and successfully advanced our cause, were we interested in the condition of those who were still racialized? Did solidarity still seem necessary? Once we had called ourselves colonized in our own country, stressing our political rights, what did we make of the discourse of Indigenous peoples on their stolen lands?⁴

The contradictions inherent to the Quiet Revolution and Quebec's movement for independence are flagrant. How can we pretend to liberate ourselves, to decolonize ourselves, to write ourselves into the narrative of emancipated peoples, while this liberation rests on the renewal of historical relations of domination and the racisms that feed them?

Decolonizing Québécois Decolonization

In present-day Quebec, what is made of questions of liberation and decolonization? What, if anything, can be salvaged from the inheritance of the 1960s to the 2000s, from that period's failures and contradictions, its cultural, legal, economic, and political archive? A genealogy of "masters in our own house" is necessary now, more than ever, as a means of returning to the past to re-orient the present. Such a genealogy will not be accomplished by the nation-alist historian, with his mission of edification; rather, a genealogy of "masters in our own house" requires the tools of a philosopher of affect and the strategy of dialectical constellation.[5] In our return to the past, we must question the origin and purpose of this slogan. We must track and critically examine its many deployments – including its extension into the present.

This task of critical examination is urgently required in order to mobilize collective work on the question of what is at stake in Quebec's liberation, today. If we are to take this question seriously, any consideration of our in-heritance of the phrase "masters in our own house" must occur within the frame of North America's settler-colonial history. We must acknowledge our shared condition of belonging to collectivities that are embedded, whether by will or by force, within the logics and relations of domination stemming from settler colonialism. At the same time, we must keep in mind that this shared colonial condition rests on the continuous construction and mainte-nance of differentiating and hierarchizing categories of population, categories we reproduce on an everyday basis: settlers, women, slaves, First Nations, fran-cophones, anglophones, workers, immigrants, the racialized, queer folks, refugees, etc.

Further, a critical perspective on settler-colonial history must deconstruct the very concept of a nature that is separate from humans and appropriable as a resource, as well as the particular configuration of social relations that results from this conception. Colonialism, as Malcom Ferdinand eloquently demonstrates from a Caribbean perspective, is both a destruction of humanity and an ecological catastrophe.[6]

Our contemporary social reality, already shaped by a global colonial in-heritance, is also witness to a proliferating biopolitics. This biopolitics repro-duces, evolves, and mutates, through the operation of a complex assemblage of what we might call *dispositifs* of dispossession.[7] These *dispositifs* are visible in the arcana of official power as it exercises legal right, but also in popular culture and the organization of production. We are shaped, fractured, and traversed by *dispositifs* of dispossession; they both empower us and subject us to arbitrary power. Their activity is not neutral: they block attempts to share in common, and they blindly reproduce structures of domination.

Collective struggle against dispossession and for decolonization necessitates a renewed attempt at understanding, critiquing, and dismantling these *dispositifs* in all of their systematicity and perpetuation of the polymorphous relations of domination. As Rosa Pires has explained, Quebec, in acceding to the status of a modern, industrial nation, elaborated its own regime of exclusion. This regime requires a critique of its own:

> Having endowed itself with its own regime of citizenship, with all the attendant inequalities based on categories of sex, gender, class, ethnicity, and race, Quebec has engendered its own Québécois mode of production of exclusion and inclusion ... Why is it that racialized immigrant women are perceived as making demands for special social rights when they simply aspire to full citizenship? Must they make special proof of their humanity, especially when they wear the veil? The Quebec state claims to be a model of interculturalism for other immigrant societies but it does not have the courage to examine its own failures.[8]

Let us take seriously the question of whether we sought "to end economic exploitation or to become the 'Boss,' as a people?" and let us add that any theorizing of dispossession from a decolonial perspective, with reference to Quebec, must have no truck with patriotism. Rather, the starting point must be that of taking on the histories which were not of our choosing (whomever we may be), and which, in the chaos of the present, we inherit in differential, unequal ways. Let us face the ethical tensions inscribed in any political action in this situation, marked by specific, complex power relations: in the tenacious gears of these relations, some of us, as we know, benefit at the expense of others.

The integrity, "survival," and political future of the Québécois nation constitute neither the starting premise of this conversation nor the *sine qua non* condition of collective engagement on the question of our shared situation. Rather, it is one issue among others (while certainly, a historically and politically important one) and it must be open to radical questioning. To insist otherwise would be to put decoloniality at the service of the national project of Quebec, in other words, to square the very circle from which we are trying to free ourselves.

My concern is thus not that of a Québécoise determined to avenge the British capture of the French enclave in the Americas (there is a whole history to that project). It is rather to participate in the ruination of the structure of settler colonialism, by assuming the ambiguous, grey position that history has delivered to me. I want to listen, to acknowledge, to join the indefatigable chorus rising from the margins to name power relations and dream of an ancient, untrammelled liberty.

And so I address my question to everyone, situated in this place, at this moment, at any particular point on the surface of the settler-colonial structure: how can we find exits, invent passageways, work to subvert the complex, contemporary structure of dispossession that is the legacy of Franco-British[9] settler colonialism? How can we sabotage the *dispositifs* of accumulation-through-dispossession that define this structure? How, especially, can we articulate all of the struggles for emancipation – decolonial, anti-racist, feminist, abolitionist, ecological – working in a materialist horizon against the erection of barriers between peoples, but without thereby ignoring the singularity of sites, affects, temporalities, and narratives which animate our shared space?

We can start by learning to narrate ourselves and our histories in a different mode, a mode of conspiracy among the living, against all the forms of accumulated power – working with whatever we have, concretely, and with generosity. The essays making up this book are intended as a contribution to this effort.

• • •

In the first part of this book, entitled "Politics," I contribute to a genealogy of the phrase "masters in our own house" through two essays on settler colonialism and the question of the decolonization of Quebec. The first, "Psychopolitics of the Colonized Québécois," addresses the relation between emancipation, history, and settler colonialism in Quebec through the conceptual pair of the colonizer/colonized, endeavouring to map decolonial passageways. On the one hand, the essay reactivates a picture of diversity and subalternity in the history of the settlement of the Saint Lawrence River valley; on the other, it issues a call for an examination of the treatment of Indigenous territory in the making of contemporary Quebec. The second essay, "Buccaneer Nationalism: A Case History," first returns to anti colonial thought in

Quebec in the 1960s in order to explore its lacunae and draw out their possibilities. Then, by way of the political writings of the activist-anthropologist Rémi Savard from the 1970s and 1980s, and testimony about this period by the writer-geographer Jean Morisset, the essay returns to sovereigntist Quebec's failures to build alliances with Indigenous peoples as it attempted to emerge from British imperialism. These two essays are followed by "Two Constitutional Notes": in the first part of this essay, I consider the idea of decolonization in contemporary Canada/Quebec; in the second, I turn a critical eye to the narration of the sovereigntist adventure of 1980 to 1990.

The more personal essays of the book's second half, entitled "Narratives," invite the reader along on some literary wandering through Quebec's settler-colonial imaginary. The essay "A Trip to Frontier Town" analyzes a family photograph dating from the early 1960s, taken on a visit to Frontier Town, a Western theme park in the American Appalachians. I use this excursion as an opportunity to explore the politics of settler-colonial representation in America. The second essay, "The Paupers of Settler Colonialism," takes up the figure of the "*mauvais pauvre*" from the poet Hector de Saint-Denys Garneau[10] (as interpreted by Yvon Rivard), and applies the figure to the Québécois colonial mentality. Through the connection that the figure of the pauper provides between the settler and poverty,[11] I move into the oeuvre of the historian and Wendat philosopher Georges Emery Sioui. In the final essay, "The Eye of the Master (Animal *Excursus*)," I consider the imaginary of the "master" in franco-Québécois literature. The master's eye emerges as a central trope of modern colonialism: he sees all, controls all, owns all. His project is productivity, production for the sole purpose of accumulation.

The question I elaborate in the course of these essays – without pretending to be able to answer it – is that of the possibility of another gaze, another eye. Throughout, I experiment with another possible disposition, available to those of us living here, and now.

• • •

I wish to thank Amélie-Anne Mailhot, Lyse Boily, Jocelyne Laflamme, Rodney Saint-Éloi, Yara El-Ghadban, Maxime-Auguste Wawanoloath, Jean Morisset, Georges Emery Sioui, Pierrot Ross-Tremblay, and Emilie Nicolas for having read all or some of these essays, and for their generous comments. I am of course solely responsible for the arguments made in this book.

PART ONE

......

Politics

I

Psychopolitics of the Colonized Québécois

Yelling "masters in our own house" in open Montagnais (Innu) territory,
is absolutely disgusting!
Louis-Edmond Hamelin[1]

The position of Quebec in the history of the colonization of the Americas is singular, owing to the complex process of settlement in the Saint Lawrence River valley. In order to undertake a genealogy of "masters in our own house" we must return to the history of French Canada, and critically re-examine the representation of the so-called "original" French colonial population which has dominated the narrative of Québécois liberation. This narrative has insisted that the "French Canadians," that is, the population descended from the French colonization of the banks of the Saint Lawrence, a population forming just one part of the Québécois today, is a *colonized* population. Let's examine this claim more closely.

The *Canadiens* of the eighteenth century, who had been inhabiting, surveying, and wandering across the American continent for close to two hundred years, were a population created by the European settler-colonial project. This enterprise was enabled by international negotiations and by the tools of legal capture tied to the Roman-Westphalian right of conquest – the Treaty of Paris of 1763 and the Royal Proclamation, issued the same year.[2] Through the treaty, the population of *Canadiens* that had been subject to the French colonial government saw itself resubjected to the English colonial government, through military conquest In the process of elaborating its status as a people, then, the francophone population passed from a population required for the purpose of settlement in the name of the French king – all those in-dentured workers, soldiers, *filles du roi*, prisoners, exiles, slaves, and settlers who were called the (old) *Canadiens* – into a population colonized by the British Empire. They were to become the "French Canadians," a population whose theatre of operations was reduced to the Laurentian enclave of the British "Province of Quebec." The old *Canadiens* played no part in these mil-itary and political negotiations. Neither did they have the benefit of any in-stitutional representation as a collectivity (notwithstanding the Catholic clergy's subsequent solicitation by representatives of the British regime, hardly a political representation worthy of the name). From hence issues the colo-nized status of a (largely) European population, colonized in the New World. This was the condition of colonization (including that part operated by the clergy) that the Quiet Revolution sought to end. This change of status in the heart of settler-colonial geography is central to the narrative recounted by those who first proclaimed themselves Québécois. It is the basis for the pre-tention to "mastery" in and of "our own house."

And yet, this image received from Québécois historiography, focused on the figure of the colonized French Canadian, represses the other part of the Québécois settler-colonial equation, through which those French Canadians who became Québécois claim their own piece of the colonial pie as a Christian and European people (that is to say, as Catholics and francophones), exercising the biopolitical prerogative of the despised English colonizer in their own name. According to mainstream Quebec's interpretation of its own history, from the 1950s Quebec assumed the colonizer's right of conquest. "We are French, transplanted to America," the line goes, staking out a project to claim and defend national territory. What the figure of the colonized French Cana-dian also represses is the whole project of spiritual conquest that took place through the missionary branches of the Catholic church. This was to construct the "missionary French Canada" of Lionel Groulx,[3] who worked toward the evangelization of the so-called "savages" of North America. This project of spiritual conquest significantly implicated French Canadians in the running of Indian residential schools in Canada and the United States and also justified missionary endeavours in the Caribbean, Africa, and Asia.[4] In spite of this implication, there is an insistent claim to the very suffering constitutive of the colonial subject: we say that we have been forced to submit, legally and po-litically, to the british-canadian continuum.

Thus, a sort of epistemological blockage marks political discourse in Quebec, producing the ambivalent posture of the settler/colonized subject. From this posture issues the dominant interpretation of Québécois liberation and the majority culture's claim to an "own house." This ambivalence, expressed at the end of the 1960s in Pierre Vallières' application of the phrase "*n—blancs*" to French Canadians, has marked the movement for liberation in a lasting way. It explains the movement's warping (the exclusionary and xenophobic edge it developed in the 1990s), as well as its current paralysis. It also represses, although never completely, an alternate figure, the people as "Boss."[5]

Neocolonialism, Quebec-Style

In Quebec, the thought and practice of settler colonialism, and the associated idea of "the North," has a long history in regions beyond the Saint Lawrence River. As is evident in the activity of the provincial minister of colonization (1888–1973),[6] there is a history of French Canadian and then Québécois settler colonialism, which stretches from the nineteenth-century settlement of the Laurentians to the claiming of the Saguenay valley and the Côte-Nord,[7] to the later settlement of Abitibi. The "mastery" of "our own house" found popular expression in the course of the new conquest of the North inaugurated by the Quiet Revolution. The slogan's popularization was in step with the construction of Quebec's hydroelectric infrastructure, the linchpin of the modern settler-colonial process. As Stéphane Savard puts it:

The 1960s and 1970s were the theatre of an immense exploitation of the hydroelectric resources of Québécois territory. These were the decades that saw the construction of gigantic hydroelectric complexes in the northern regions of Quebec, its peripheries: the Manicouagan-Outardes complex in the backcountry of the Côte-Nord (1959–1978), the Churchill Falls project in Labrador (1966–1972), and the complex along La Grande River in James Bay (1971–1984). These projects also provided the occasion for the promotion of specific symbolic and identitarian representations by Hydro-Québec and Québécois political players, notably that of a Québécois technological modernity that would conquer the towns and the industries of the Laurentian valley.[8]

The concept of a Québécois territorial mastery ties in with a wider project to capture and industrialize all of the natural resources in the frontiers of the "Province of Quebec," while at the same time imposing in this northern space an institutionalized Québécois presence, in French. Each of the most evocative political figures in the history of modern Quebec successively associated himself with the conquest of what was called (not very equivocally) "*Nouveau-Québec*": Maurice Le Noblet Duplessis,[9] who died in Schefferville while a guest of the Iron Ore Company, in the middle of Innu territory; Jean Lesage[10] and René Lévesque,[11] who fully realized the power grab that was the nationalized exploitation of hydroelectric power, putting the power of a provincial state, benefitting from all the jurisdictional prerogatives of the Canadian Constitution, behind the corporate occupation of the great rivers of the James Bay and the Côte-Nord; Daniel Johnson Sr., who launched the Manic-Outardes project in the 1950s;[12] Robert Bourassa,[13] who, only when his hand was forced by the Cree, negotiated the James Bay Agreement in the 1970s; Bernard Landry,[14] who completed this historic cessation of Aboriginal title, facilitated by the terms of a british-canadian legal order; and finally Jean Charest,[15] who launched the Plan Nord[16] to reboot the Québécois economy through the exploitation of mineral resources in the unceded territories of the Algonquin, the Atikamekw, and the Innu.

If the passage of social power from the Roman Catholic Church to the Québécois state represented the first leg of the Quiet Revolution, and thus the concrete expression of Québécois political thought, the colonization of *le Nord* for the benefit of the provincial state represented the second. "Masters in our own house" spoke of the imposition of Québécois government authority, administrative structures, and official language from the Côte-Nord to Nunavik; it also announced a considerable land grab – relatively belated in view of the history of the colonization of the Americas – founded on an inherited European right of conquest.[17] As Caroline Desbiens writes:

> Paradoxically this colonial vision of *le Nord* was inscribed precisely within the movement for the decolonization of the Québécois, which took hold during the Quiet Revolution. In their attempt to ameliorate their economic condition and take hold of the reins of government, francophone Québécois, who formed the majority in the province, treated

the Indigenous lands in the north as a southern colony. Considering James Bay to be *terra nullius*, provincial political and economic actors sought to universalize their vision of the world and its resources in order to install the mechanisms of exploitation that would bring profit to the South.[18]

Modern industrial Quebec, the Quebec we have inherited, the Quebec which we are – which claims the whole of a provincial territory whose parameters were established through federal law in 1912, the Quebec of the slogan "masters in our own house," is a colonial state. The release from the constitutional bosom of royalist Canada, which was anticipated by the official drivers of Quebec's sovereigntist project, did not constitute a real decolonization, a genuine political, legal, economic, and moral rupture with the structure of Franco-British dispossession.

What was realized in this sovereigntist gesture was rather the kind of colonization, on behalf of a particular historical group, that the world had seen previously in American independence and in all the other white independences accomplished in the Americas. By means of the same manoeuvre, the Québécois assumed the mantle of rightful colonizers, a mantle which they believed themselves to have held under the French regime and lost with the British "Conquest." From this point on, they imagined, they would join the company of independent nations of the New World, whose "foundation" consisted in the replacement of European colonizers with "local" or "creole" ones. What a legacy. Zebedee Nungak provides an Inuit perspective on Quebec:

> No one would question the "masters" part of the slogan if the frontiers of Quebec delimited the places where the descendants of Champlain lived and worked the land in order to maintain and nourish their distinct French identity, their language, and culture in the ways that they wished. The problem is with the "our own house" part, which has come to encompass Eeyou Istchee (Cree territory) and Inuit Nunangat, great swathes of territory where there is not one ounce of French history or language or culture. These lands should never have been folded into the French "our own house." But that is exactly what happened when Quebec went headfirst into its James Bay Project.[19]

In light of the evolution of Quebec through the Quiet Revolution, the question today – more than ever – is what does it mean to be a master? What does this political aspiration to mastery signify? And perhaps most urgently, what is the geometry of this "our own house," which seemed to carry a kind of self-evidence in its poetic and political invocations from the 1960s through to the 1990s? From the perspective of the twenty-first century, and one that stands in solidarity with immigrants, Indigenous peoples, racialized people, and queer communities, that self-evidence no longer holds.

This fact may sadden those who wish to make Québécois history by channelling an unreconstituted national affect belonging to another era. However, nothing less than a total re-examination of our values is required. This is clear to all but the most obtuse, and most unitarily marked by a morose political sensibility after the successive failures of Québécois nationalism. The re-examination of our values must begin by critiquing the interpretation of history that serves as a foundation for the project of national liberation. The received narrative is a sclerotic one. Recent political events provide a painful illustration of this fact: one has only to think of the adoption of the Act respecting the laicity of the State in 2019, or the Quebec government's reaction to the activism of hereditary Wet'suwet'en chiefs during the winter of 2020.[20]

Stop Thinking like a State

The enactment of a local decolonial imaginary is going to require opening up the fault lines at the heart of the collective narrative of liberation, the vehicle for the slogan "masters in our own house." We must have the courage and confidence to examine these fault lines, and to draw on the ethical forces and bonds of a decolonial imaginary. To this end, I propose two paths of reflection, which I pursue in the course of the following essays through a number of different modalities.

Revisiting the Ethnogenesis of Québécois Nationalism

There is a presumption woven through the received narrative of Québécois national liberation that suggests today's francophone Québécois, descended from an "original" French colonial population, should inherit the French colonial prerogative that was appropriated with the British "Conquest" of 1760. According to this version of history, the pretension of the majority of Québécois to national sovereignty retains something of the sovereignty that absolutist France would have exercised in America, by virtue of a European right of conquest. This population retains part of the dream of French settlement in the New World. The negotiated maintenance of Roman Catholic institutions and the Civil Code serve as evidence of this continuity, as does the purported extinction of Indigenous rights by the French in New France (particularly in what was called the *Domaine du Roy*), all of which were affirmed by English colonial right and upheld by Québécois jurists. And yet, when one examines the details of the constitution of this "original" French colonial population, the filiation is shaky. It is characterised by *epistemic murk*, or muddiness, to borrow the expression used by Michael Taussig to describe the way the European colonial state roots itself in the Americas.[21]

The population installed in the Saint Lawrence River valley in the seventeenth and eighteenth centuries, in the period of New France, and from which a part of the population living in Quebec today descends, was in the main not made up of the kind of colonial political subjects one would call *entitled* (those who actually were entitled returned to France with the Treaty of Paris, if not before). Rather, the population of those who stayed behind following the departure of the colonial elite were those whom present-day Canadian law refers to as "populations settled to support the aims of colonialism"[22] – in other words, they were an unskilled workforce, mobilized in the service of the colonial enterprise. They were, for the most part, what the historian Peter Moogk has referred to as "reluctant exiles."[23] It is by means of this involuntary exile and mobilization that the history of French Canada as a colony inscribes itself in the wider history of French colonization in the Americas – in Acadia, the Great Lakes, Louisiana, Sainte-Domingue, Martinique, Guadeloupe, and Brazil.

The settler populations mobilized for this French enterprise were made up of groups of varying geometries and states of relative dispossession: in the case of New France, temporary and long-term workers, domestic servants, day labourers, fishermen, *coureurs de bois*, interpreters, soldiers, monks and nuns, boatmen, artisans, fur trade workers, *filles du roi*, wives, children, tenant-farmers, "domesticated Indians," enslaved Indigenous peoples and Africans, exiles and European prisoners, creolized populations, landless people, seasonal Indigenous occupants of the river banks, squatters, refugees, hermits, questors, travellers, witches, eaters of squirrel and racoon, marginal folks, horsemen, *alouette*.[24]

To be sure, the peasant class of tenant-farmers who gradually became the class supplying the indentured workers and soldiers in the French colonies presents the picture of a homogenous and relatively autonomous French colonial society, one which benefited from a certain material comfort, according to the norms of the period. It was also a white population. At the same time, some economic nuancing is required: as Christian Dessureault notes, "the peasant egalitarianism of the old rural world of the Saint Lawrence valley is a *frontier myth*. The peasants were not only characterized by their level of wealth, which was not negligeable, but also by their relations to the field of production."[25]

Furthermore, while one might insist with a certain boastfulness on the relative material comfort of the French settlers in this era, and depict a Laurentian seigneurial regime that might seem a sinecure in comparison to the feudal institutions of France,[26] nevertheless, under the French regime the peasant class had neither political rights, nor literacy, nor capital, and very little decision-making power in relation to the means of production. This is why it was possible to *de facto* transfer the population along with the land, from French to British rule.[27] In spite of their relative material comfort, these white settlers were also largely illiterate, in apparent contrast to the biblical literacy of English settlers in southern regions.

The remarkably differentiated and dispersed geography of the French presence in America was repressed by the creation of the "Province of Quebec"[28] and by the British geographical imagination more generally. Even in the twentieth century, this dispersion remains evident in the presence of francophones not only in Quebec, but also Acadia/Maine, Manitoba, Ontario, New England, the area south of the Great Lakes, Louisiana, Oregon, Western Canada, and in small communities from Cape Saint George in Newfoundland to Fort Smith and Fort Resolution in the Northwest Territories. Within this rather stunning territoriality, there is an extremely diverse mosaic of French vernaculars, a complex heterogeneity, and a relatively persistent territorial and maritime mobility. The diversity I refer to is not just an "ethnic" one, although this dimension is part of it, and it is poorly represented in the historiography centred on Quebec as an enclave within British territory. It is a diversity that demands a radical reconsideration of the nativist notion of authentic, home-grown Québécois (or Québécois *de souche*) both within the history of the "French" presence in America and within contemporary Québécois thinking about immigration.

What is certain is that from the point of view of France itself, the initial settler population in the valley of the Saint Lawrence was without entitlements. "France abandoned us," it has long been said here. Indeed, for both French and British colonial agents this population was simply a form of fixed capital awaiting mobilization, although it was also, from their various perspectives, insubordinate, backward, or misunderstood. The *Canadiens* who experienced the change of colonial regime, and from whom a portion of Québécois are descended (myself included, I am told, with documents proffered to prove it), belonged to a subaltern population: they were sort-of-francophone, but they were not "French." In the words of Jacques Ferron:[29]

There's Cartier, there's Dollard des Ormeaux,[30] there's the Conquest: everything we could ask for, but it's not our story. Notice that I do not disdain the national literature and historiography: it contains the wisdom of nations, the great wisdom of the world. It is just that if one's drawing on it, one should be honest. That's not where our account lies; rather, it's in the Banque d'Hochelaga or the Caisse Populaire Desjardins.[31]

It is too simple to view this history through the unitary lens of French origins, and say that the Québécois were colonizers who were then, at a certain moment, colonized themselves. The initial settler population was a people only by default, a "bastard" people made up of indentured labourers, the low-born, workers, and their dependents. Later, this population would hoist itself to the status of modern colonizer, through the relentless but ambiguous efforts of a little nineteenth-century entrepreneurial elite, which became a clerical one draping itself in a "French" aura in the early twentieth century, and then a bureaucratic and cultural one beginning in the 1960s. An improbable *Reconquista*, this modern colonial feat was accomplished on the basis of a right of conquest in the Americas, upheld by elite European legal *dispositifs* of dispossession (the state, capital), and through the support of a motley, oral people, a people-by-default, made up of popular classes of various means, variously humiliated.

In this regard, the revolt of the Patriotes in 1837 to 1838,[32] the Front de libération du Québec (FLQ) in the 1960s,[33] the attempts by the Parti Québécois (PQ)
to set in motion a negotiated sovereignty in the 1980s and 1990s, the Act respecting the laicity of the State recently adopted by the Quebec government
(banning the wearing of the veil by those in positions of public authority),
but especially, from the beginning of the Quiet Revolution, the industrial and
administrative conquest of the territory referred to as the "Province of Quebec": each of these participates in the dimension of Québécois liberation that
rests on the claim to being authentic, homegrown Québécois, to being *de
souche*, a dimension that seeks to retain colonial power in order to ground a
claim to Québécois sovereignty. This is the agency of the people as "Boss." As
Robert Bourassa put it at the beginning of the 1970s: "Developing James Bay
is a way of leaving the valley of the Saint Lawrence, widening our frontiers
and taking possession of our resources."[34] *Pace* Ferron, this is the cultural fund
that takes the form of a bank account.

A veritable case of *pharmakon*,[35] the Quiet Revolution was supposed to
bring about access to the dignity associated with the position of colonizer, the
owner of the ensemble of *dispositifs* of dispossession. It was supposed to provide a taste of the dignity of the master and heal the wound of subalternity
(as well as the servitude that induced that condition). It was about taking back
"our" rights as a European people, the assumed right of whites in the Americas. This is the nationalist "we" of the Parti Québécois of Pauline Marois in
2014, a "we" that, failing the achievement of an independent state of Quebec,
wanted to affirm the ethnocultural primacy of the descendants of the "original" French population, fantasized as a homogenous group. Today, it is this
post-sovereigntist neonationalism that is in favour. The political party forming government (Coalition Avenir Québec, founded by a former sovereigntist
of the PQ[36]) identifies itself with the interests of the historical majority of
French extraction at the heart of the Franco-British regime of dispossession
that is modern Canada. This, in a nutshell, is the Québécois version of "masters
in our own house" – hardly a vehicle of emancipation. As Emilie Nicolas has
written:

Through a confusion and reduction of the dynamics of class – seen as
the labour of the capitalist colonial project – and the dynamics of race
– that which had to be annihilated so that "civilization" could advance

– we wound up coming up with some strange ideas about the history of Quebec. And I find myself, like many others, in the absurd position of having to demonstrate that, in a British empire in which ideas of race and religion played a central role, those of French origin were treated like whites and Christians. Poor, inferior, but still white. Catholic, unfortunately, but still Christian.[37]

The old *Canadiens* who did the handiwork of French colonialism – at least, those who did not desert the cause, take to the woods, embrace their subaltern destiny, or rebel against empire and any other kind of nation-statist enlistment – necessarily played a part in the relations of domination specific to imperial racism, in order to carve out a little European kingdom for themselves. A contrary reading simply does not stand up to analysis.

Why is the story that we tell ourselves, here in Quebec, the one that belongs to a privileged ethnic group in control of a colonial state? How might we embrace a story based, rather, on the constitutively motley, oral, subaltern history of the old *Canadiens*, a story based on the diversity involved in settlement, and the insubordination to empire? How might such an alternative story nourish the sense of a shared continental history, of which we continue to be a part, here and now?

Foregrounding Indigenous Territoriality

In order to arrive at a decolonial movement that might nourish, and in turn be nourished by, the diverse, local emancipatory affects percolating within the space of empire, it is crucial to foreground Indigenous presence in those territories placed within the jurisdiction of the province of Quebec, approximately 90 per cent of which have the title of *domaine de l'État*, the Québécois equivalent of Crown lands.

A large portion of the territory over which the government exerts its authority was never ceded, in the sense recognized by the neocolonial britishcanadian regime. The peoples who endure the Plan Nord, notably the Algonquin Anishinaabeg, the Innu, and the Atikamekw, seek (and in some cases have been seeking for several decades) to reach agreements that would spell out their rights and obligations in their traditional territories. Equally, they seek to enforce sectoral agreements ignored by successive Quebec governments. Attempting, through various means, to address the spirit of Canadian law on the duty to consult, they seek to be heard at the heart of consultation processes. Despairing of success, they also have sought reparations and compensation for the expropriations they have endured. And yet, Canadian courts and successive Québécois governments consider settler access to territory north of the forty-ninth parallel, its occupation by populations "required for the purpose of settlement," and the exploitation and capitalization of aquatic, hydroelectric, forest, mining, maritime, and tourist resources, to constitute relevant "compelling and substantial public purpose[s]."[38] This legal pretence, justifying incursion on Indigenous territories, might be extended to Franco-British colonialism itself, as well as the very fact of the state apparatus of the province of Quebec, which continues colonialism today in the name of the francophone majority holding the reigns of power, having emancipated itself from a certain kind of subalternity.

Even if Canadian and Québécois governments went ahead with a series of treaties according to the established practices of modern treaty agreements, the result would be, in part, the consolidation of Crown sovereignty and the generalized project of colonial extraction for the benefit of the owners of the means of production and stockholders, their rentier dependents. The legal and financial trade-offs negotiated with Indigenous groups in these contexts (groups which are authorized to negotiate by the state itself), including the renunciation of the inherent right to the territory implied in this type of treaty in almost every case, constitute an irreparable loss of sovereignty for all Indigenous peoples within an extractive, dispossessing economy. In order to unravel this structure, the starting point must be acknowledgement that Quebec plays the role of – in fact, it is a signal instance of – the dispossessive colonial state.

Jean-Jacques Simard articulated this pragmatically in 1995, as he took account, in a very attenuated way, of the effects of the James Bay and Northern Quebec Agreement[39] on the lives of Cree and Inuit peoples:

> Words count, at the end of the day. Even if the fundamental objectives of the James Bay Agreement bore some relation to today's concept of "governmental autonomy," those words do not appear in the agreement.

In my opinion, for what it's worth, the significant difference is a whole conceptual progress achieved since then, such that we now suspect it really is about founding governments and radically altering the established political order, rather than simply emancipating bureaucracies and playing around with detailed programmes to "respond to the needs" of populations.

We are starting to grasp that renewing the relationship between Indigenous peoples and the rest of the country has to be based on the constitutional model, rather than just references to that great reformist document, the James Bay and Northern Quebec Agreement, or similar forms of agreement between the state as "Boss" and specific clienteles.[40]

In order to think about a genuine horizon of emancipation in Quebec, it will be necessary to reinterpret the momentum toward independence associated with the phrase "masters in our own house." In a "compelling and substantial" way, we will need to rethink the relationships between peoples across this provincial territory, the modalities through which its borders are held together, the manner in which we draw our subsistence from it, and the powers of dispossession we uphold (and which uphold us) as we do so.

An emancipatory politics, framed from this perspective, cannot economize on these difficult questions, which fundamentally challenge the way of life of the majority and the legitimacy of the claim to mastery over national territory that is associated with that way of life: extractivist, privatizing, founded on accumulation. These questions require critical work on the colonial political imaginary and at the same time, generative work to build political thought based on alliances.

Who Needs a Master?

Colonial history offers numerous examples of national liberation by the state and capital, which have culminated in the same result we have seen in Quebec: the self-dispossession of peoples through the exercise of nation-statist privileges within a global economy, and the rerouting of oppressions toward other subaltern populations and minorities.

The trajectory of Québécois liberation, anchored to the idea of becoming "masters in our own house," was forged not just through modern Canada's establishment of sovereignty in the nineteenth and twentieth centuries and in the context of a concrete historical and political situation, but also through the power of a progressivist colonial imagination. The point here is not to produce judgements of the past. More productively, it is to read the ambivalent legacy of Québécois liberation, one of the grand political experiments of the twentieth century, for the missed opportunities for solidarity that still might hold potential for a new cycle of decolonization. One may wish to reply that the ethical, political, and epistemological values of Québécois resistance created a distinct site of power within continental colonial space – even if that resistance assumed colonial institutions as its model for emancipation – and thus should not be dismissed. The creation of that site of power is not what is at issue here. It is on the very basis of this system of actually existing sites that it is possible to rethink liberation in a more complete and inclusive way today. But the retracing of our steps must be radical and we must not compromise in the face of Quebec's continental, colonial, historical, and economic situation. For example, it is going to be necessary to rethink our geography on the basis of the material, relational, human linkage of Roxham Road,[41] to think passageways and barriers together, indeed, to identify passageways within barriers.

For those who identify as "majority" Québécois to access a whole other way of thinking about independence in North America, for them to inaugurate a different way of living, according to a chain of solidarity based on the spirit of alliance, they first must embark on a process of psychopolitical and material disidentification. What is required is nothing less than disidentification from the colonial state and the capitalist, extractivist, dispossessive way of life which that state implants, supports, constantly renews, generalizes, and legitimizes. We must face head-on our actually existing relations with other peoples in this territory, the origins of those relations, and their ontological and legal frames.

Facing up to the relations of domination that have constituted our history, including the violence exercised in the name of cultural survivance and national affirmation, is a considerable challenge for a population that has always had difficulty understanding itself as plural. The challenge will be especially great because this population's very existence is intimately linked to the European colonial enterprise. As a basis for coherence and collective action, it has no ancestral traditions, no inherent territorial rights that do not already benefit from the political aura of European colonizer and the prestige of nineteenth-century independencies. At the same time, the population lacks connection to the ethical force of actually existing decolonial and anti-racist mobilizations. But this very situation of placelessness within territory, of lack of access to power, on the part of a population whose archaic segment descends from a servile, residual population with neither social mobility nor possibility of representation, is also an opportunity to think otherwise about possession and dispossession, to unravel colonialism, to invent other ways of living, and embrace an in-betweeness constituted through humility and hospitality.

The Québécois political question for the twenty-first century will not be how to discover the route to finally becoming "masters in our own house," which would only complete the European colonization of the Americas in "our" name. Rather, the question will be how to think and act in relation to the compelling and substantial goal of abolishing, via a historical alliance, all of those relations of servitude that compose the Franco-British form of dispossession that we have inherited, in a differentiated manner, whomever we may be.

How, then, to live without a master, collectively, in a sustainable way, in the Franco-British colonial territories we inhabit?[42]

2

Buccaneer Nationalism:
A Case History

You will ask, how is it possible to consider as natural ally a people of whom
certain unhinged elements come and fight right beneath our eyes, and the eyes
of our mothers and fathers?

Rémi Savard[1]

When we examine Quebec's independence movement with the benefit of
hindsight, it is almost revolting to realize that not only the movement itself
but the historiography that it engendered virtually ignores Indigenous presence. Even if we pay special attention to the movement's anti-colonial texts
from the 1960s, Indigenous presence is at best anecdotal in them. Sean Mills
has written on this score, in his *The Empire Within: Postcolonial Thought and
Political Activism in Sixties Montreal*:

> Throughout the early to mid-1960s, virtually all of Montreal's radical
> francophone writers, reading their society through the lens of an anti-
> colonial theory that highlighted the Manichean nature of empire,
> internalized these divisions while ignoring the possibility that the
> Aboriginal populations in Quebec could have their *own* claims of
> colonization, their own grievances, and would eventually develop their
> own terms of resistance.[2]

In the 1960s of which Mills writes, any mention of the Indigenous question
in connection with the Québécois anti-colonial struggle is rare and operates
to efface, while mining the concept of Indigeneity, in the interests of the

francophone/Québécois demand for decolonization. Either Indigenous peoples are seen to have disappeared (such were they victimized by British colonialism), with any residual communities seen to be de facto slated for rapid vanishing and the political margins (Mills cites the writer and director Jacques Godbout as evidence for this perspective[3]), or Québécois writers summarily set themselves up as the inheritors of a historical métissage[4] and a colonial suffering which Indigenous peoples experienced first (as asserted by the Beauceville-born Raoul Roy,[5] a precursor to the nationalist movement of the 1950s; other writers, André Major included,[6] claim Indigenous ancestry).

A Decolonial Breach

Mills tracks the rare, politically supportive reference to Indigenous presence in Montreal anti-colonial thought in the 1960s and 1970s. He notes that Vallières, in his L'urgence de choisir (1971),[7] asserted that Indigenous peoples were more oppressed than French Canadians in Quebec, returning via this claim to his writings of the 1960s, which, in their history of British colonialism in North America, assigned Indigenous peoples only a slight and folkloric place. In the years that followed, Vallières – the same Vallières who, it must be stressed, had always entertained a certain distrust of the promotion of nationalism as the end of Québécois struggles (a distrust already evident in the 1965 manifesto of the Mouvement de libération populaire)[8] – would support Indigenous sovereignty claims and underline that their colonization and genocide was the result of those he called "our European ancestors."[9] During the so-called Oka Crisis in 1990, Vallières vigorously defended the Mohawk perspective, amidst a generalized animosity.[10] Mills also recalls that Léandre Bergeron, of franco-Manitoban origin, proposed the seeds of a more egalitarian perspective on the Indigenous question in his Petit manuel d'histoire du Québec in 1970, in which he explored the "complexities and multi-layered nature of colonization in Quebec, and ... discusse[d] the marginalization of Native populations in the province's past."[11]

As for the revolutionary and felquiste[12] Charles Gagnon,[13] who addresses neither Indigenous politics specifically, nor the intricacies of French and British colonialism in "Feu sur l'Amérique," an essay in which racism is one of the main axes of analysis, he nonetheless considers the place of Indigenous struggles in his revolutionary struggle against imperialism and capitalism. The young Gagnon writes:

> The national liberation struggles for which this continent is soon to be the stage will be truly meaningful only in this context [of anti-racism]. It is not about, and should not be about, turning Quebec into another Mexico, politically "independent" but economically exploited, pillaged, and dispossessed. It is not about creating one or more black or amerindian capitalist state and submitting to imperialism. It is about destroying imperialism and racism; constructing a new society in North America in which different races and different ethnicities will live together harmoniously because each one will be given the structures and institutions that it deems favourable to its own realization.[14]

The liberation of Indigenous and Afro-descended peoples is considered on an equal footing with Québécois liberation. For Gagnon, as for other anti-colonial thinkers and political leaders since Louis Riel, the goal of revolution is for oppressed groups to be able to govern themselves and live side by side.

In the same era, in "Les têtes à Papineau," Gagnon's analysis of Quebec's situation addresses the reactionary element of the nationalist movement, which, in his view, does not aim to question the established order but rather to deploy that order in its own interests. The analysis seems strangely contemporary and resonates with the critique that "masters in our own house" thinking requires today:

> There is no lack of progressive forces in Quebec, but they are almost all reactionary! Progressive, because they sincerely seek to ameliorate the fate of the mass of workers or a group more or less of the same size; reactionary, because the goals they have set themselves, and in the process, the means they use, do not really endanger the established Order.[15]

If the critique does not explicitly address the colonial relation between French-descended Québécois, Indigenous peoples, Afro-descended peoples, and longstanding and recent immigrants, it nonetheless clearly anticipates the Nordic neocolonialism of the 1970s and the grand schemes for becoming "masters in our own house" discussed in the previous chapter. The critique also anticipates the identitarian and right-wing turn of sovereigntism which, having seized the state apparatus for its own ends, would construct its legitimacy in opposition to minorities and immigration.

And yet equally, one finds strong, although marginal, positions being taken on behalf of Indigenous struggles in Quebec in the 1970s and 1980s. The work of the geographer Jean Morisset, *Les chiens s'entre-dévorent… Indiens, Blancs et Métis dans le Grand Nord canadien*,[16] is a milestone in contemporary decolonial literature in Quebec.[17] The book is based on the report of an inquiry into the sociocultural impacts of the construction of the Mackenzie Valley Pipeline in Dene territory in the 1970s. In this study, originally commissioned by the Government of Canada, Morisset gives voice to thirty interview participants, letting their testimony be his guide; the work produces its own placed-based and relational theoretical frames. Between the lines, the text stresses Dene presence on their land and unveils the face of modern colonialism in the way the Canadian government ensures the conditions for economic development of the northwest. Francophone-Indigenous solidarity is here put into practice: taking up the critique of the Mackenzie Valley Pipeline project, Morisset offers an equally virulent critique of the Québécois approach to the development of James Bay.[18]

To this brief list of intellectual and political alliances between Québécois and Indigenous peoples, one also must add the two-month strike of teachers in Nunavik in 1972 in support of Inuit demands for the protection of their cultural rights. Mills writes of a report by the province's teachers' union, entitled *Le Nouveau-Québec, ou comment des colonisés traitent leur colonie…*,[19] which concluded that Indigenous cultural rights claims were being treated differently from Québécois ones:

[The report] argued that Native populations lived differently from southerners, and had different ways of conceptualizing their past and future. Francophone Quebeckers – "themselves profoundly oppressed in the economic and political spheres" – needed to become conscious of "the colonialist treatment which they are inflicting upon groups of Indians and Esquimaux." The province's teachers' union articulated the distance separating it from the modernizing goals of the Quebec state:

"Against the right of states to organize peoples," the union maintained, "we propose the right of peoples to organize themselves."[20]

The potential for a decolonial alliance between Québécois(e) workers and Indigenous struggles, as illustrated in this little-known strike, the memory of which is now virtually effaced, was also apparent to the Métis activist Howard Adams, who in 1975 wrote:

It is understandable that Indians and Métis identify more with the colonized colored people of the Third World than with the white working class of their own nation. Instead of struggling against capitalism, the majority of workers are inclined to accept it as the best of all possible systems; they believe it only needs to be reformed so that they will receive greater privileges and benefits. Those workers who have become integrated into the capitalist system are not at present a potential source of support for revolutionary change. There are exceptions, of course: many workers and unions in Quebec are in the forefront of struggles against the capitalist system. Nevertheless, there comes a time when all oppressed people must join together in a united struggle and form a new revolutionary class. It appears that this new class will comprise women, youth, natives, and workers. At the same time, the ruling class must be prevented from isolating any one group from the remainder, as they did in 1885 and again in 1970 during the Quebec crisis.[21]

Adams identifies a parallel between the crushing of the 1885 North-West Resistance, which ended with the political assassination through hanging of the Métis leader Louis Riel, and the use of the War Measures Act in Quebec in 1970 to put an end to the decade-long political troubles which culminated in the kidnapping of two political figures, James R. Cross and Pierre Laporte, and the death of the latter. Québécois(e) workers in this era were seen as an exception to (white) North American reformist unionism, their struggles potentially linked to the anti-colonial Indigenous and revolutionary struggles in what was called the "Third World."

In this review of exceptions to the rule, it is crucial to stress the monumental work of the Laboratoire d'anthropologie amérindienne de Montréal,[22] founded in 1969, which included José Mailhot, Sylvie Vincent, Rémi Savard,

Madeleine Lefebvre, Claude Lachapelle, and Joséphine Bacon.[23] The work of this group on linguistics, oral literature, and social and political questions related to their Innu contemporaries was unprecedented in Quebec and continues to represent a concrete, politically engaged legacy of Québécois decolonial thought.[24]

In this regard, the work of the Québécois anthropologist Rémi Savard stands out as a persistent antidote to the forces that would erase the Indigenous question within the independence movement. He pointed to these forces of erasure as well as the political and ethical blockage they produced at the end of the 1970s:

> We still refuse to admit that there is a whole botched chapter. This is due to our failure to affirm, clearly and precisely, that our own difference is predicated upon an equally clear and precise recognition of theirs, and of the common destiny connecting us to this north-eastern peninsula of America. Sooner or later, this work is going to have to be done.[25]

Notwithstanding the nuancing that this declaration may require, and even if it seems a bit premature or even futile at this stage in the evolution of relationships between Québécois *indépendantistes* and Indigenous peoples, it seems that, fifty years later, we are still, *mutatis mutandis*, at the same point.

Savard launched a challenge to his contemporaries in the 1970s and 1980s that is still relevant. It was Savard who, on the eve of the first referendum on Quebec sovereignty, observed that racism still pervaded Québécois society. He wrote: "What we must therefore start to say to one another, above the heads of all the exploiters, is that power itself needs this kind of flourishing racism, in order to do its demoniacal work."[26] This statement contains a whole theoretical and political program calling for the articulation of critiques of the different forms of dispossession operating at the heart of the historical and contemporary colonial machine that is post-British Canada.

Thus it is important to return to the sites of Quebec's historical failure to encounter the Indigenous world, as these were documented by Savard. The *crux* of this failure is between 1971 and 1981. That is the junction at which possibly irreparable harm was done to the relationship between the Québécois and Indigenous peoples, the point at which Quebec chose to go it alone in its struggle against federal political domination, explicitly and unequivocally joining forces with the very empire that was supposed to be dismantled, thereby fully donning the role of modern colonizer.[27]

Returning to the missed opportunities for intersecting struggles in recent history might permit a more holistic understanding of the state of relations between Québécois and Indigenous peoples. This return might also provide the basis for thinking about the legal transformations and political strategies that would create the conditions in Quebec for a new attempt at the great circle of free peoples in northeastern America. Because, in the still timely words of Savard: "As long as our disputes with Indigenous peoples are not resolved on the basis of a reciprocal equality, we will not succeed in fully defining ourselves as a people."[28] One might add that it will be impossible to unsettle the structures of exclusion that reproduce xenophobia, racism, and anti-immigration politics unless we place Indigenous issues at the heart of political life in Quebec.

From Eyou Istchee to Wet'suwet'en Territory: Rethinking a Political Posture

In broad brushstrokes, early sovereigntist Québécois thought on Indigenous issues is deeply uninspiring, but hardly surprising given the tenor of the different "crises" and confrontations that have unfolded between Indigenous and Québécois peoples since the era of resistance by the Cree in James Bay. Whether one thinks of resistance by the Inuit in the Arctic; the salmon wars of the Innu and Mi'gmaq in the east; the Oka Crisis at Akwesasne, Kahnawake, and Montreal/Tiohtiake; the blockade by the Innu of the construction of La Romaine in Nitassinan/Côte-Nord; the claims of the Algonquins of Nitaskinan/Barriere Lake or those of the Atikamekws in Nitaskinan/Mauricie; or more recently the demonstrations in support of Wet'suwet'en traditional chiefs opposing pipeline construction on their territory in northern British Columbia, in every case, from the beginning of the 1970s until the present day, Indigenous peoples appear to the francophone majority as an obstacle to the liberation of Québécois/Canadians.

This suspicion of and outright opposition to Indigenous political struggles on the part of the Québécois has its roots in the project of economic modernization and cultural affirmation of French Canadians, a group described as underprivileged and discriminated against in the 1969 report of the Royal Commission on Bilingualism and Biculturalism.[29] Savard was right to imagine, in the era of the sovereigntist movement's solidification, that Québécois opposition to Indigenous claims was linked to the fact that they themselves were injured by the Canadian constitutional regime: "When it comes to the Québécois population, which has not itself achieved a political regime in its own image, it has often taken the path of supporting its own rulers in opposition to the Indigenous peoples of Quebec."[30] It was, in a sense, in a spirit of competition, even envy, that Québécois asked themselves: why them and not us? Or even: why them before us?

In fact, it is still common to hear, in the mouths of Québécois political thinkers and actors, the idea that Indigenous political interests are a barrier to aspirations for independence or development in Quebec. It is an old idea: in the era of the grand construction projects of James Bay, it was said that Cree claims were the business of the federal government; the most worked-up of these commentators even spoke of Ottawa plotting against Quebec.[31]

But as Savard knew, it is not Ottawa that promotes Indigenous political affirmation in Canada – the case is the opposite. The White Paper of Jean Chrétien and Pierre Trudeau in 1969[32] sought to abolish Indian status and devolve responsibility for Indigenous services to the provinces. This strategy amounted to eliminating Indigenous peoples by means of cultural genocide and "progressive politics," renouncing recognition of the numbered treaties signed in the nineteenth century, and denying the existence of unceded territories. This federal government initiative was met with organized Indigenous resistance, some of the products of which were the creation of the Assembly of First Nations (AFN) and the Indians of Quebec Association (IQA), which later became the Assembly of First Nations of Quebec and Labrador (AFNQL).[33]

From the 1970s – before the James Bay issue and the federal approach to comprehensive land claims beginning in 1973 – the IQA insisted on the unceded status of numerous Indigenous territories in the province, as well as the provisions related to unceded lands in the Quebec Boundaries Extension Act of 1912 (which folded parts of Rupert's Land within the province of Quebec, excluding coastlines). The 1912 Act called for treaty making to obtain surrender of title in the event of development in the Arctic.[34] In short, Indigenous peoples have asserted their rights on their traditional territories within Quebec in opposition to the colonial vision of the government of Canada, and it is thanks to intense and costly mobilizations that they have been able to make their voices heard, in a struggle that continues today.

For historical reasons, the greatest portion of unceded territories in which Indigenous peoples can still assert ancestral title lie in the provinces of Quebec and British Columbia.[35] Natural resource development requires provincial involvement in negotiations over the use and sharing of territory. The federal government is often involved as well, its agents never lacking an appetite for political control over the provinces, and especially over Quebec. To be sure, limitations on the exploitation of territory have impacts on "job creation" and "economic prosperity" for Québécois, especially in the so-called regions. These impacts have mobilized working-class Québécois against Indigenous claims in recent decades: in these confrontations, the industries by which they live – forestry, mining, construction, and tourism – are necessarily at stake.[36]

In the obligation to negotiate, Québécois sovereigntists and other economic nationalists may see a constraint, an obstacle, even a federal plot. But from another point of view, it is possible to see in this obligation an opportunity to rethink the Québécois political posture within federal and continental space, to reimagine the way we live on this territory, the way we define it, and, at the heart of all of this, how we conceive of collective wealth.[37] The obligation to negotiate could also be seen as an invitation to a radical repositioning of ourselves in relation to Indigenous presence and everything that presence implies. This repositioning might be informed by a critical version of the tradition of decolonial thought in Quebec. But the political history of recent decades indicates that this door, when opened, has been systematically closed. Let us examine this history more closely.

The Parti Québécois before Indigenous Claims

The election of the Parti Québécois in 1976 marked a turning point in the course of "masters in our own house" and the assumption of political power by the Québécois within the British Empire. An explicitly sovereigntist government was installed in Quebec and now took the reins of the provincial state. Today, it is hard to imagine the power of that moment for the descendants of the old *Canadiens*: that illiterate, residual people, descended from the *water boys*,[38] speaking a bastard language, and subjected to the pressure of British-Canadian history explicitly aimed at its docile submission and cultural assimilation. Now, that people had acceded, in its own name, to the pinnacle of institutional power, the state. This people without a state had proven to the English colonizer that it was worthy of a state and belonged in power. It was a heroic feat; it was revenge; it was a whole new world coming into being, an inner victory as well as a victory against what had appeared to be the tide of history.

In this context it is all the more interesting to pause over the Indigenous policy of the first *péquiste*[39] government of René Lévesque, in order to examine Quebec's colonial relationship to Indigenous peoples. The anthropologist-activist Savard had a front row seat and closely documented the actions of the sovereigntist government, whose quest and ideals he shared. At the same time, he was quickly forced to conclude that Quebec under the first mandate of the PQ had positioned itself in alignment with British colonialism. Savard wrote:

In the spring of 1977, on the airwaves of Radio-Canada, Minister Bérubé hesitatingly proclaimed his government's official, definitive opposition to any recognition of the rights of Indigenous peoples to self-determination, explaining that this was inconceivable, since "we are the owners of the soil."[40]

Minister Yves Bérubé was responsible for Natural Resources, and Lands and Forests, and what he was defending in the face of Indigenous peoples' sovereignty claims was clear: the Québécois strategy for achieving mastery through economic development *en français* would be founded on the exploitation of natural resources. This control over natural resources would be supported by claims to "ownership of the soil," referring to the title or "domain"[41] of the provincial state and drawing opportunistically on the letter of the British North America Act: it was a provincial matter, according to the otherwise despised Canadian Constitution.[42] In the feudal model, the domain refers to the lands a *seigneur* retains for leasing out and direct cultivation, as distinct from those lots that his dues-paying tenants, the *habitants*, work in their own name.[43] It is from the domain of the state that the status of public lands descends. As it happens, the unceded Indigenous territories of the north-east are almost entirely situated on such public lands, which make up almost 90 per cent of the provincial territory of Quebec. The statement of the *péquiste* minister is explicit about the nature of the control that the Québécois intended to assert by means of their "national" government: we are the *seigneurs* of these public lands and no politically based claims to these lands will be entertained. This was Québécois sovereignty in action; other claims were merely domestic, necessarily secondary within the framework of the Quebec state.

The next year, Savard recalls that Gérald Godin,[44] who, in *péquiste* hagiography appears as the champion of "openness to the Other," reiterated "with even more forcefulness the *péquiste* approach to the Indigenous file."[45] The *péquiste* position, which would define the approach in the coming decades, was clear: it drew on a right of conquest inherited from the British Crown. In other words, as Savard regretfully concludes, the sovereigntist project was explicitly committed to the genocidal program of the federal government "of which the *Québécois* people itself, frequently, had been the object."[46]

The colonial posture of the first *indépendantiste* government in the history of Quebec contains a clear economic motivation and founds itself in legal conservativism and opportunism. This posture would provide the model for relationships between the state of Quebec and Indigenous peoples. Today, one can see that this politics, besides being inconsistent with the *Québécois* discourse of liberation and not even minimally meeting the criteria for collective rights claimed by Indigenous peoples on the international scene from 1920 to 1950, was the starting point for a series of missed political opportunities. By means of these failures, largely unnoticed in their time but more apparent today, the new Quebec marginalized itself when it came to Indigenous issues. This was the predictable result of its much sought after economic and cultural "normalization." In this way Quebec botched its political coming of age in America; it blew its opportunity to ensure that its birth was a contribution to the emancipation of all.

Below I briefly turn to three moments in sovereigntist Quebec's missed opportunity for an encounter with Indigenous peoples.

The Château Frontenac Summit

Savard tells of a particularly painful event representing a key moment of what we might term flattened decolonialism. It consists in a summit of the members of Lévesque's government and representatives of Indigenous nations held at the Château Frontenac, in Quebec City, on 14 and 15 December 1978. There is a powerful symbolism to this event. The nation-to-nation meeting took place on the very site of the old Château Saint-Louis, the seat of the governors of New France and then of British military conquerors. It was ground zero for settler colonialism in North America. Of equal significance was the fact that this was the first convening of the historical peoples cohabiting the valley of the great river of Canada: the Indigenous peoples and the Québécois, at least to the extent that the latter could legitimately consider itself a people, through its election of a Parti Québécois government. The Indigenous leaders were present at this meeting as the representatives of "sovereign nations," recalls Savard. They came to the meeting against the advice of the federal government, which did not relish the formation of a politically independent franco-Indigenous space (recall that this was just eight years before the government of Pierre Trudeau invoked the War Measures Act to crush the Québécois revolt).

Savard, who was present at the meeting, reports that the Indigenous leaders asked Premier Lévesque, very directly, how he understood the equality between Indigenous and Québécois peoples. "Do you foresee the same sovereign status, for us, which you have demanded from English Canada? And do you address us now as your equals or as your wards?" they asked.[47] The vague or insulting answers offered by representatives of the Québécois state caused a number of Indigenous participants to leave the room, Savard reports. The front page of Le Devoir, from 16 December 1978, described the treatment of the Indigenous chiefs: "It was an exchange on the topic of Amerindian rights beyond the reserve that broke down the fragile discussion between the members of government and the 135 participants invited by the Québécois state to renew an official dialogue which had not existed since 1701." Quebec clearly announced that it intended to substitute itself for the paternalist and colonial federal government and did not have in mind a partnership, a collaboration in independence, with Indigenous peoples. It is important to note the ellipsis

in the account provided by *Le Devoir*, which represents the *péquiste* government as descending from the French colonial regime that presided over the
Great Peace of Montreal in 1701.[48]

Savard depicts a moment that is shameful for Quebec and for the sovereigntist movement in particular. His first-hand witnessing sets the moment against
a background of ill-prepared government, and describes how it resulted in
displays of ignorance and suspicion on the part of that government. And yet,
Savard adds, "it was not a government made up of fools!"[49] Morisset, who
was also present at the Château Frontenac meeting, notes that while both the
fact of the meeting and the creation the same year of the Secrétariat des affaires
gouvernementales en milieu autochtone et inuit (SAGMAI) under the direction of Eric Goudreau seemed in line with the replacement of the term
"sauvage" with "Autochtone," neither signalled any change to the deep dy-
namic of relations between Quebec and Indigenous peoples.

For Savard, all of this can be explained by a cultural colonialism on the
part of Québécois elites, one which insists on "French" lineage, the racial distinction of the colonizers, and the providential mission of French Canada as
laid out by Lionel Groulx:

> Merely scratch the surface of the thousand and one careful oratorical
> surfaces of our political men, and you discover an unmistakeable sus-
> picion of the "savages," a feeling that this Indian chief of Sept-Îles is not
> going to be permitted to speak as an equal to our leader! "Savages are
> savages!" ... No more than English Canada can we imagine a political
> solution other than the *melting pot*, at one end, and the refugee camp,
> at the other.[50]

Either Indigenous peoples assimilate as Québécois and put themselves in
the service of the economy, or they will be excluded from the political and
territorial reality of the new Quebec: the settler-colonial mentality (which
also has been called whiteness[51]) is incapable of thinking beyond such a view.
The Quebec of this era seems to have been incapable of thinking of its independence other than through a hoarding of the position of master. The posture is identical to that held today by identitarian nationalism in relation to
immigrants: either you assimilate or you will be excluded from citizenship.
Neither is it very different from the posture found among lettered French

Canadians of the early twentieth century, even if it deploys a different vocabulary. For example, in *Notes sur la Côte Nord du Bas Saint-Laurent et le Labrador canadien*, published in Quebec in 1927, one reads:

> Here is all that remains of a once powerful nation; perhaps next we shall see its last representatives disappear, but if such a sad fate should prove to be inevitable for this race, one might say that at least they met a fine end.

> Protected in every material way by the federal government and through services provided on reserve, from a religious point of view they are also attended to by means of the tireless efforts of the Catholic missionaries on the coast. Today, all of these Indians, without exception, are fervent, practicing Christians. In converting them to Christianity, in giving them as much material comfort as possible, even if the transition from savage to civilized life seems to them irredeemably fatal, we repay this nation, once a loyal ally to our ancestors, the enormous debt of recognition we owe.[52]

As Minister Bérubé put it in the context of the summit at the Château Frontenac, according to Savard: "From now on, you will live within society." We find here, fully illuminated, the idea that assimilation (into industrial modernity, into Christianity) is a gift to colonized peoples – the repayment of a debt incurred in the process of colonization. The inevitable disappearance of Indigenous peoples is declared, as well as the impossibility of their pursuing their own way of life, according to the "vanishing Indian" ideology circulated by classical anthropology. This idea of survival through assimilation also may be found in the work of Jacques Ferron at the end of the 1970s. He writes to his sister, Madeleine Ferron, in reply to her report of having met Aurélien Gill, chief of Pointe-Bleue/Mashteuiatsh, who would participate in the Château Frontenac summit the following year: "I have never been in favour of their artificially sustained survival, financed by the federal government in order to create problems for us. I have simply wanted to say, we have partially assimilated them and they have no salvation other than through us."[53] This is the "progressive" position on the Indigenous question that is most commonly found among the sovereigntists (and, in symmetrical fashion, the one applied

to by Canada to francophones). There is no indication that leaders of the Parti
Québécois ever thought otherwise.

The Extended Hand of the Indian Brotherhood

In an attempt to console ourselves, or to justify the missed encounter at the
Château Frontenac, it may be tempting to contend that on the part of Indigenous leaders, there has never been an openness to recognizing the Québécois
struggle for sovereignty, that they have always acted in accordance with their
positioning in relation to the federal government as a fiduciary. (The argument is replayed today in relation to immigrants who are seen to be "federalists," by default.) However, the opposition to Québécois sovereignty in the
1970s and 1980s context was neither unanimous nor entrenched.[54]

In fact, as Savard reports, in 1978, two years before the referendum on Quebec sovereignty, Noel Starblanket,[55] president of the National Indian Brotherhood (the NIB, which became the Assembly of First Nations or AFN in 1982),
wrote to Lévesque:

> We have studied your project of sovereignty-association. This political
> platform suits us because it coincides with the demands of the Indians
> throughout Canada who want to exercise the greatest possible power
> over their natural resources and establish normal relations with their
> neighbours. We are starting from a position that is the opposite of yours:
> you are in Confederation and you want to step outside of it with one
> foot, whereas we, who have never been part of the confederate club, want
> to set foot within it. In practice, however, we are in complete agreement.
> Let us take hands. Together, let us tear off the federal colonial hold. But
> let us do this on behalf of our respective collectivities, rather than putting
> the Indians under the thumb of another white power, in this case, that
> of Quebec and the other Canadian provinces.[56]

A hand is clearly being extended by the most visible, broadest federation
of Indigenous organizations in the country. Referring to the sovereignty-
association proposed by the Parti Québécois, the NIB president affirms on
behalf of his organization that "this political platform suits us." The subaltern
position of francophones within the Canadian regime is recognized; their

existence as a collectivity is a given. Starblanket proposes an alliance between Quebec and First Nations, against the colonial power of the federal government. The precondition for this alliance is equality: Quebec, in its struggle for independence, will not be permitted to replace the federal government as colonizer. It will have to work at the parallel liberation of Indigenous peoples and the dismantling of the British North America Act, by and for those francophone and Indigenous peoples whom the Act minoritizes. It is a testament to the poor understanding of the continental colonial situation, on the part of the sovereigntist elite of the era, that these two events, the extended hand of the NIB and the meeting at the Château Frontenac, were unable to found another approach to Quebec's independence, and that the NIB's invitation to alliance should have remained a dead letter. The sovereigntist elite's weak analysis evinced a deeply engrained racism, bent on the profits of industrialization.

A Challenge to the People of Quebec

Another opening toward alliance between Indigenous peoples and the sovereigntist government of Lévesque appeared with the repatriation of the Constitution. The repatriation process led to the adoption of the Constitution Act of 1982, the product of an agreement that excluded Quebec, in the end, but, as the result of extensive mobilization and pressure from Indigenous leaders, added Section 35(1), recognizing the existence of inherent title wherever treaties had not been signed, on the basis of the Royal Proclamation of 1763.[57]

It is Morisset who recalls this forgotten episode in the history of the sovereigntist movement in his *Sur la piste du Canada errant* (2018). Two important Indigenous leaders spoke out in the context of the preliminary agreement between the premiers that excluded both Quebec and Indigenous peoples. They underlined the injustice of this double exclusion. The words of George Manuel,[58] former chief of the NIB and president of the Union of British Columbia Chiefs, were reported in the *Globe and Mail* on 7 November 1981:

> [Manuel] said that the agreement reached by the premiers and Prime Minister Pierre Trudeau on Thursday was unjust and placed the Indians in the "garbage bins of Canadian history." "But we are a firm, fierce and

proud people. We will fight back … It is very depressing to think that after all these years as a country, when the chips are down it is the Indian people and the Quebeckers who are brutally ripped off by the majority," Mr. Manuel read from a one-page statement that shook constantly.[59]

Several days later, on national television, Georges Erasmus,[60] who was then president of the NIB, issued an explicit invitation to alliance, as had Noel Starblanket before him. Erasmus called for an alliance between Indigenous peoples and Quebec in order to counter Ottawa's strategy for repatriating the Constitution without recognizing minoritized peoples:

We Native peoples, along with Quebec, have been swept under the carpet of the country that Trudeau has just constituted with his companions from the English-speaking provinces. I call on the government and the people of Quebec, and on René Lévesque in particular, to make their reaction known and express their feelings about Native peoples' rights to self-determination.

I challenge the people of Quebec – if, in fact, this people believes in self-determination – now is the time to support Native peoples. It is not the time to remain separated from one another and steer ourselves, individually, to defeat. Now is the time for action. The hour has come. We the Native peoples need the support of Quebec in the coming hours. We need the support of the Québécois people.

The country is in a state of national emergency that requires Native peoples and Québécois to come together.[61]

The question would be debated in a meeting of ministers at Quebec. The dismissive response of the *péquiste* government was voiced by Godin, who provided the following justification (as quoted in verbatim, by Morisset).

Quebec can sympathize with Indian nations' demand that their rights be recognized in the Constitution of Canada, but from there to draw the conclusion that there is an alliance would be dangerous for all parties to such an alliance. Because recent experience has shown us that one is played against the other, and basically, yesterday's allies are more divided than ever today...

So I think we will each wage battles on our own territory – on our own legal territory, each on our own terrain...

The federal government, in this case, will use every means to divide potential allies. And this is the reason why we'll no longer play this game. We hope the Indians score their point, that they obtain precise and specific recognition of their rights in the Constitution of Canada...

I absolutely agree that Aboriginal rights should be inscribed in the Constitution of Canada, just as I think they should be in the Constitution of a sovereign Quebec.[62]

Morisset met with Godin immediately after he made these remarks. Godin justified the remarks by referring to Indigenous peoples' anti-Québécois sentiment and betrayal of the Québécois cause. It is evident that Godin and the Parti Québécois harbour a rancour toward the Cree and the Inuit for stringently opposing Quebec's sovereignty-association project in 1980.

Morisset, for his part, interprets this disavowal as a tragedy for francophone existence in America:

In that urgent context, Quebec's unresponsiveness effectively endorsed Ottawa's coup d'état, through the set of fairly weak and contradictory responses discussed here. With this disgraceful rebuff, leaving Ottawa with all the power and authority with regard to the Native question and ... the Québécois question, a unique opportunity was shattered – no doubt never to be seen again – for the demeaned *Canadiens* and the Native peoples to finally provide their shared interpretation of the history of Canada and *British America*.[63]

Pierre Trudeau claimed to be "decolonizing Canada" through the repatriation of the Constitution, even while reinscribing the terms of the colonial relation with Indigenous peoples in this new pact; meanwhile, the Québécois claimed sovereignty on the basis of their experience of colonial wrong, even as they became Canada's accomplices through their unresponsiveness to Indigenous invitations. They demonstrated their preference for a colonial posture and their suspicion of Indigenous self-determination.[64] If there was any remaining doubt, the rupture between decolonial thought in Quebec and the sovereigntist movement became decisive at this moment.

Savard identifies the Québécois colonial mentality at work in this failure to become the allies of Indigenous peoples. Parodying the reasoning one might attribute to Godin, he writes:

> Must we become the allies of *savages*, right when we are on the verge of convincing the world that we have become a *normal* and *civilized* people, as our premier, René Lévesque, is at pains to repeat? Will we have gone to such lengths to explain to Europeans that we no longer wear feathers, only to risk becoming the victims of this sorry confusion of races? At most we hear people asking themselves if it's worth risking the future of a francophone collectivity, whose culture has proven itself viable, by allying ourselves with peoples we know to be outside of history.[65]

A question is exposed here, and it remains to this day: Why is it that, in the Québécois elite's republican imagination, allying ourselves with Indigenous peoples (and with feminist and anti-racist perspectives, and the queer imagination, and multiculturalism) would hurt the emancipation of francophones? Why should it have to be one or the other? Why should there be this competition between emancipations, if it is not that Québécois republicanism actually does not aspire to the abolition of all servitude, since that would rob it of the elusive position of master?

Buccanneer Nationalism

Savard, in an argument close to Morisset's, is categorical about the conditions of possibility for francophone political existence in America:

> As for the Québécois project of self-determination itself, I think that it has no chance of having its day in court, either in the short or the long run, unless it articulates itself to the pan-Indigenous dynamic … The

greatest disservice we could do our descendants would be to underestimate the political significance of Indigenous aspirations and the continental scope of this vast political awakening.[66]

Quebec's independence can never be simply the republican project of a francophone majority. It must be able to contribute to a liberation conceived much more widely than it has been up until now (that is, as francophone cultural survival through the economic exploitation of Indigenous territory). Its contribution will be meaningful only if it can understand its own position as contingent, and legally and politically specific.

What Charles Gagnon characterized as reactionary in the Québécois nationalist movement, Savard, thinking about the Indigenous question more specifically, characterized as "buccaneer nationalism":

To certain of our citizens, Indigenous aspirations to political autonomy seem to be an occasion for raging against the threat posed by the creation of *holes* in our own national territory. This is the *canadian* edge of our nationalism, a bit *buccaneer*, we might say. To the delight of the federalists, it is also what prevents us from seizing the historical opportunity that Indigenous peoples could hardly be offering more explicitly.[67]

This suggestive figure of buccaneer nationalism brings us back to the time of French colonial settlement, and the French occupation of the Caribbean in particular. The "buccaneers" were those groups of veterans, failed settlers, navy deserters, and shipwrecked and tired freebooters, who were French, Dutch, and English, and who lived through hunting and smuggling in the colony of Saint-Domingue (which would liberate itself from France, becoming Haiti in 1804). These rag-tag cosmopolitan groups were, in a sense, cousins to the first *Canadien* populations – in particular the mythical *coureurs de bois* of Old Canada (those men of the *chasse-galerie* versus the *chasse-partie*).[68] The buccaneers were tightly connected to freebooters, the maritime version of themselves, and they skirted the coasts of Spanish America looking for opportunities to ransack, pillage, and plunder Spanish colonial settlements. Thus, of Jean-David Nau, a native of Poitou who was indentured in the Antilles and then went from being a buccaneer to a freebooter, we read that he was famous for acts of cannibalism, among other things: "Nau would rip out a man's heart and eat it, while it was still quivering, in order to sow terror in others."[69] The buccaneers and freebooters were floating populations, without attachments, without the title of colonizers; they occupied Caribbean space in a sporadic, ghostly way, cultivating a colonial know-how and exerting an ambivalent form of violence, partly in the name of French occupation and partly for their own gain. They were much like the *Canadiens* hired for the fur trade and other voyageurs who travelled those colonial routes of North America – the northwest, the Oregon route, the Louisiana route.

This arc between Quebec and the Caribbean evokes the commerce around the Atlantic more generally, including the transportation of indentured workers, *filles du roi*, the slave trade, and the routes between Saint-Domingue, Old Canada, and France. It reminds us of the discoverer-entrepreneurs, of French neo-mercantilism, of the very idea of *terra incognita*, through all of which plunder verges on genocide. Savard puts us on the trail of a delicious parallel between the buccaneer-*coureur de bois* and contemporary Québécois who would conquer vast Indigenous spaces: fear of the fragmentation of territory (which one occupies without real legitimacy); men (especially men) more or less voluntarily exiled, linked to the land through their contraband practices and animated by the taste for "spoils"; suspicion of Indigenous peoples; a courting of and sometimes implication in the slave trade; and ferocious competitiveness with other colonizing groups. The buccaneer figure evokes the seeking of easy profit: the raiding of northern natural resources that has defined Québécois modernity, from Manic-Outardes to La Romaine, for example.

• • •

In the context of renewed Indigenous struggle in Canada, including Idle No More and the chain of connected blockades contesting oil and gas development on traditional territories, the door to the creation of alliances among equal partners may reopen. There may be a real opportunity for postcolonial justice in encounters that are inclusive, transformative, communal, and open to transvaluation of post-British ontological and legal frames.

We must equip ourselves with the tools to conceive of such equality and such a transformation of perspective. This will require more than just political will (since that only begs the question), but in fact a whole "epistemic displacement."[70] This displacement demands that we think differently about the conditions for the liberation of peoples on this territory. The question is not how to secure the territorial sovereignty necessary to the destructive capitalization of natural resources for the enrichment of a particular, exclusive group, nor is it a matter of arriving at a deal among parvenus. Rather, it is how to share this nourishing territory, in an intrinsically plural manner, while collectively and inclusively taking on the challenges that this sharing entails: it is to dream of a transcultural decolonial order. For once, to encounter one another in living sites,[71] rather than the sites of power.

3

Two Constitutional Notes

The vision of Quebec proposed by the advocates of both independence and Confederation – which have become indissociable, in any case – has well and truly failed. It's time to move on to something else.

Jean Morisset[1]

Territory Versus Sovereignty

Decolonization is a political principle at the heart of Indigenous self-determination struggles. The principle nourishes Indigenous collectivities and allied groups of varying practices and aspirations, ranging from the restoration of Indigenous names and the critique of cultural appropriation, to declarations of political sovereignty and the revitalization of customary rights and traditional land uses.

Decolonizing actions seek to attenuate, or better still, undo, the imposition of a legal, political, economic, cultural, epistemological, and spiritual frame of reference by the British Empire, other European powers, and successive colonial governments in North America. They are about dismantling the structures that contemporary Canada and Quebec have inherited, state institutions that take concrete as well as diffuse, intangible forms. But of all the consequences of empire, the most haunting legacy is territorial dispossession.

Decolonization requires that we rethink collective life in terms of the sharing of territory, taking the lead from Indigenous peoples whose place-based histories, knowledges, and practices are so sophisticated in this regard. Working out this ethical cohabitation will be the task of political collectivities of varying geometries, each having a specific, constitutive relation to this earthly habitat as well as institutions and practices reflecting the particularity of that relation.

In pursuit of such a multiform, emancipatory relation to territory, and the alliance building and openness to new ways of living that are going to be necessary along the way, we might begin with a thought experiment. Imagine – *just to see what might come of it* – letting go of two ideas, often thought to be indispensable to emancipation, even as they paradoxically reinscribe the very terms of colonialism. The first is the idea of the nation, intrinsically tied to the idea of the state and a colonial relation to territory. The second is the idea of property, an idea that inhibits our very ability to imagine an egalitarian and emancipatory relation to territory.

The concept of sovereignty upon which Canada-Quebec is founded implies that the legal existence of the territory and its ultimate possession (*imperium*) derive from the "Crown,"[2] a fictive entity inherited from the British monarchy and imposed in America through the Royal Proclamation of 1763. Through this document, the British Empire reserved sovereignty over all of North America for itself and unilaterally subjected both the Indigenous peoples and the *Canadiens* (to use the vernacular), a now-minoritized francophone population. It assigned the former an "Indian territory" and enclosed the latter within an enclave along the Saint Lawrence, between Montreal and Quebec. Planting the populations required for settlement through an explicitly racialized scheme and within a predatorily mapped geography, the British Empire set in motion the conjoined projects of settler colonialism and racial capitalism.

This eighteenth-century territorial imaginary is the scaffolding for Canadian sovereignty. The legal and political framework it established for the British colonial enterprise in the eighteenth century would be renewed in the nineteenth century with the numbered treaties, and then again in the twentieth century, with the modern treaties signed between Canada and Indigenous peoples. This framework was also renewed in the course of the struggle of (those who became) the Québécois, for political recognition within (or on the outskirts of) the Canadian federation.

The lesser, non-sovereign formations called Quebec and Indigeneity were officially delimited in this context, but they were also shaped by the flows and traces of refugees, migrants, indentured and temporary workers, and displaced peoples – by their histories, accidents, crossings, and encounters over a geography of coasts, lakes, valleys, and industrial towns. All of these landscapes and pockets of peoplehood would be caught in the snares of Confederation and thereby rendered invisible. As the history of the British North America Act reminds us, not every collectivity, language, or art of living is reflected in the form of state sovereignty, that crystallization of the absolute power of the tyrants of the Middle Ages. Even more singular is the hold on power, the monopoly on violence, that comes with being reflected in a state. And yet, inconceivable though it may seem, this power is not what everyone seeks.

The Canadian legal and political framework was also established through property law and a federal and provincial management of land titles that systematically limited inhabitants' access to land. Management of various forms of title defined by the state for Indigenous peoples, settlers, and migrants reserved privileged access to natural resources for those entities pursuing industrial exploitation. On a scale from the village to the multinational corporation, and whether for forestry, mining, petroleum, agriculture, tourism, or services, access was channelled to industry. In the process, those still in pursuit of "national" recognition were reduced to pursuing rents, salaries, and associated comforts, as well as a utilitarian relation to territory or what was now a reified, packaged "nature." From the point of view of empire, there was never any question of another kind of relation.

What would a radical reconsideration of state sovereignty, and a concomitant rethinking of our relation to territory, require?

Each of us has the right to those things necessary to the pursuit of a free existence, "each body has the right to make use of its capacities as it displaces itself across space," according to the words of an old inhabitant of the Saint Lawrence I like to quote.[3] It is this free access to the fundamentals of life, this capacity to make respectful use of things and to live in an egalitarian fashion within one's immediate, concrete context that the apparatus of Canadian sovereignty takes over and rigidifies, equipping it with specific intentions. State sovereignty in our time enforces participation in a civilization of accumulation, with all the powers of the law.

That some profit more than others from this arrangement and that it is a source of conflict are facts that shape our actual condition and they only complicate and intensify the work of imagining other possible arrangements, other possible routes. This inequality is a large part of what propels the present reconsideration of Quebec-Canada's industrial sovereignty and the bases for its specific morality – its utilitarian norm, its cartography, its cannibalisms.

But various scenarios are possible, and by and large, could cohabit. An order-seeker might say: "In view of these historical facts, any decolonization process will have multiple fronts if it is to be a decolonization for everyone. Likewise, it will require the dismantling of Canadian sovereignty so as to unleash a *radical redistribution of its sources* and a whole new relation to territory." A dreamer might say: "Decolonization could be the staging of a panamerican funerary procession for the British Crown, something like a popular opera, by a great coalition of the living." As for the leaders present at the Château Frontenac in Quebec City in 1978, they said to themselves, as they departed: "Maybe it would be interesting to hold the next meeting on a reserve, instead of in a luxurious urban hotel. Maybe this would enable the kind of encounter that words alone cannot bring about."

Indépendance as the Medium

I am a longtime fan of the sovereigntist saga, having been formed and de-formed through long years of watching Radio-Canada television soap operas by my mother's side in my childhood and adolescence. Every night of the week, in our home between the Appalachians and the Saint Lawrence River, I drank in the stories and intrigues of the characters in *Terre humaine*, *Le temps d'une paix*, *Monsieur le ministre*, *Le parc des braves*, *Les filles de Caleb*, *Les tisserands du pouvoir*, *Les dames de cœur*, *L'héritage*, *Shehaweh*, *Lance et compte*, *Scoop*, *Roch*, *Providence*... I could go on.[4]

My experience and vision of Québécois society were forged in specific land-scapes, within an "uncultured" family culture, through years of schooling, and surrounded by the René Lévesque relics with which my grandmother ornamented the walls. Television was a powerful aspect of this formation, the medium par excellence of modern Québécois culture, its advent roughly contemporaneous with the *indépendantiste* movement.

In my parents' house, television was the very heart of our shared existence; it was our electric hearth. It was on television that I watched the two disastrous referenda, in 1980 and 1995.[5] Surrounded by family, at the age of six I listened to every word of René Lévesque's 1980 concession speech and retained, above all, the tone of infinite sadness. In 1995, on election night, a group of friends

gathered in my apartment on la rue du Roi in Quebec City to follow the coverage. We had all voted yes and we experienced the same sadness as in 1980.
In the bloom of my CÉGEP[6] years, I discovered newspapers, especially Lise
Bissonnette in *Le Devoir*. In their pages, I followed our fantasmatic adventure
in the world of states:

- the soap opera of *Lucien and the flesh-eating disease* ("Let us
  continue!");[7]
- the *Money and the ethnic vote controversy*, starring *Monsieur*, all
  boozed up on the referendum stage;[8]
- the adventures of André Boisclair: cocaine, nightlife, and limousines;[9]
- Vidéotrongate on the Hill;[10]
- the repeat political take-offs of Parizeau's said-heir, that musician-
  financier;[11]
- Péladeau-the-son at the wheel, his rise and fall;[12]
- the "Jeffersonian" moment of Bernard Drainville, father of the
  "Charter of Values";[13]
- and so on.

The last episode in the all-time greatest series of reality TV Quebec was
the March 2019 defection of a young *péquiste* deputy from the south shore
of Montreal. Along with her went the status of the Parti Québécois as
second party in Quebec's National Assembly. A "loser" party, anyway, for
Catherine Fournier, a figure one might associate with the *ti-pop* tendency.[14]
She fled the party under cover of darkness, as though sneaking away with
the keys to the family car, to meet up with the American sons of the
wooden-legged patriarch, Lucien Bouchard. "Dad, you're a *loser*," his sons
told him, agreeing with his own courageous self-assessment, as Bouchard
reports in a recent documentary.

This all has the feel of a succession crisis, but it also demonstrates the impossibility of inheriting a legacy defined by loss, bruises, and shame, when,
after all, our experience is complicated by the basic persistence of life and the
stunning beauty of the intimately known; by class conflict, normalized daily
violence, and everyday imperial racism; and by the technicolour dreams of
distant, grandiose things – studying the classics, Florida, an Olympic stadium,
an Oscar.

This apparent succession crisis also produces the sense of awakening from a dream, as if the *indépendantiste* movement, having become sovereigntism, confused itself with its representation.[15] If the "cause" took refuge in the tele-visual imaginary, maybe this was because the "real" narrative, the one that should have unfolded – that is to say, saying "yes" to independence – was re-jected. The televisual imaginary has served both as crucible and as coffin, a vehicle for the pain, regret, and bitterness of a collective soul, denying its fail-ure and remaining aggressively blind to the roots of that failure.

• • •

The last statement by the guardians of the sovereigntist tradition, issued from inside the public-relations bunker that has called itself the PQ since Fournier's desertion, is a symptomatic one. "Everything is on the table," it declared, "except the fact that we are *indépendantistes*." This was supposed to be an act of good faith, in the midst of inflammatory provocations being issued from all directions.

But the "except" amounts to the depressing repetition of a resistance to any self-examination. To insist on the "fact that we are *indépendantistes*" is to refuse to examine anything at all, including what it would mean to imagine real lib-eration instead of simply "facing reality."

The refusal is a way of saying: move along, there's nothing here that re-quires rethinking; we've already thought about everything. All that remains is the staging of what has already been thought, in a manner that will spark the enthusiasm of spectators gathered around the televisual urns, because, in this great electrified national space, the satellites are still pointed at elec-toral districts.

But there would be a great deal to rethink if only we would give ourselves the right to do so and if only we could be open to rigorous re-examination of the "fact" of *indépendantisme*. As in the last card to be interpreted in the Celtic Cross Tarot spread, the outcome card, the loser is also the one who finds a way out.

It sometimes appears that the sovereigntists who picked up the baton of the *indépendantiste* project have forgotten why sovereignty should be pursued. It is as if they are motivated by a form of atavism, loyalty, pride, some kind of spell. If they do recall the reasons for the project, perhaps they also know that these have little traction in everyday life in Quebec and seem to be so much empty gesticulation to many. Sovereigntism is on a course to invisibility in its present form, as one big toxic sulk. No doubt this is the reason why in- stitutionalized sovereigntists have been manoeuvring around the panacea of identity for more than a decade: identity being the only idea capable of putting the word *nation* into circulation in the contemporary media landscape, and the only image capable of inflaming the desire for conquest which seems to animate political life.

The history we recount is also the story of the medium in which history unfolds. The political imaginary expressed in this history has to be cultivated, and continuously reworked, so that it speaks to the most relevant cultural codes, whatever they may be.

To radically question the *indépendantiste* positioning, to stop avoiding this question and protecting this "fact," it seems to me, is the only way to free the sovereigntist imaginary from the modes of representation to which it is captive today – I do not say "loser" modes ("loser" being a bit young for me; after all, at the tender age of seventeen, I admired the prose of Denise Bombardier).[16] I would say, rather: reified, and simplistic.

• • •

What I propose, then, is a repoliticization of the debate on independence that would take place in three fairly challenging steps:

First: there are some collective affects in need of healing. The sovereigntists of 1995 are still in a rage over the referendum. They are possessed by the fury of the patriarch who has lost his hold, but still has the stamina and the piety necessary to avenge himself before his too-numerous children (products of the large family form, that generator of superfluous beings). These uncon- trollable children must be made to understand that he needs his freedom, he needs to realize his own dreams, for his own reasons. Grandpa did not get his state. His bitterness is explosive. He hates youth even more than federalists. He is paranoid about multiculturalists and potential Brutuses. And the last set of his offspring, his neglected children – lacking an inheritance and branching off chaotically, smothering themselves in flags – are going around guarding the borders like biker gangs, firing off machine guns in mosques.

In my version of the television soap opera with a better ending, the ensem- ble of human society finally and unequivocally recognizes the historical suf- fering of that minor people of the Saint Lawrence, the product of French colonization in America, thereby unearthing some of the pain for which anger serves as a cover. This process could start with official apologies by the Government of Canada, inheritor of the British Crown, addressed to the descendants of those families who watched a thousand buildings burn on the river's south shore in the summer of 1759. There would be apologies, in turn, to the guys I went to school with, in the county of Bellechasse, taking fentanyl in their decrepit family homes by the manure-poisoned fields bordering highway 132, waiting for the apocalyptic miracle of the third link.[17] "*C'est à ton tour de te laisser parler d'amour.*"[18]

Second: we must take note of the fact that there is a political energy in Quebec that is without any specific allegiance. This spirit of revolt, a certain distrust of power, has assumed different forms in the course of the nearly half a millennium of colonial inhabitation that is called Quebec. The sovereigntist project, which was not without merit, or dignity, or romance, was one of the most original attempts to channel this energy. It was a constructive conversion of reactive sentiment. At first it incarnated itself in collective terms, as decolonization, in a variant of the democratic impulse; then, more pragmatically, as a statist dream of normalcy. This project both succeeded and failed. It "made history," in all the ways in which that phrase signals the master putting his stamp on things: witness the development of Quebec's North, the French face of Montreal, "Québec Inc."[19] and its home-grown millionaires, the improved quality of life of the Québécois, the Act respecting the laicity of the State and the (not unrelated?) fact that Quebec remains part of Canadian Confederation. The supposed fruits of the endeavour are evident, even if these do not include an independent state, and even if, as a consequence, Quebec's status remains fragile. And yet, the spirit of revolt still exists. It simply has been displaced in another direction.

What does this Laurentian fervent give rise to, today? What are its avenues? In my version of the television soap opera, the guardians of the sovereigntist tradition stop their shouting and accept the help they are being offered in giving new meanings to independence. They accept that the desire for transformation, the spirit of insurrection, and the distrust of exclusionary power nourished by our existence here, do not belong to them exclusively, that these things are not "sovereigntist" – that it is possible to take note of political energy, and attend to the ethical tensions within it, but that political energy is not something that is fabricated (at least, not without great dangers).

Thirdly: we must begin anew in figuring out what it means to "decolonize."
The French-speaking population of the eighteenth century, the social residue
of the half-hearted absolutist project of New France, was colonized by the
British Empire and enclosed within the Saint Lawrence River valley through
the Royal Proclamation of 1763. Clearly, to decolonize involves dismantling
these political, legal, economic, and cultural constraints. The most fundamental mistake of the sovereigntist movement, in my view, was to have
thought that political freedom could be achieved without destroying the colonial structures of the British Empire, including its predatory relation to territory and its structural racism. Instead, the movement imagined that political
freedom could be achieved by colonizing North America in our own name,
in French, as if to take back the torch of the conqueror, which was never ours
to begin with. "How colonial," as we used to say when I was a kid, to describe
behaviour judged to be vile, base, small-minded, hick, like some guy making
his engine backfire.

Quebec, in its struggle for emancipation and through its public utterances,
its thought, its economic, legislative, and political moves, confused the pursuit
of justice for all peoples with accession to dominant power and privilege.
Granted, this was in the context of what appeared to be immediate require-
ments and competing imperatives; that is not in question. But as to the treatment that Québécois governments have reserved for Indigenous peoples of
any allegiance, and the paranoid relation to immigration which has come to
dominate national politics in Quebec, as well as the total lack of a vision of
ecological justice for the land and the ensemble of its inhabitants, what is
there to say but: "How colonial"?

• • •

And so: how to remove ourselves from the coils of the sovereigntist televisual
imaginary? How to facilitate the free, patient coming-together of peoples
within this shared ecological space? How to live without conquest, without
plunder, without deception? If we can answer these questions, then, no doubt,
the idea of independence will live on.

PART TWO

......

Narratives

4
A Trip to Frontier Town

What is the literature of a country,
if not the trial of its civilization?
Jacques Ferron[1]

A leap into vernacular thought exposes the lived experience of inhabiting a territory, including the various stratifications and statuses that are part of that experience. In turning to a franco-subaltern imaginary, I do not mean to suggest that it is the repository of an authentic Québécois speech,[2] nor that the silenced, the poor, the *déclassés*, the *joual*-speakers,[3] and the regional inhabitants provide us with a more ethical discourse. Rather, my interest is in the evidence of diversity, divergence, singularity, and multiplicity in this cultural layer; the possibilities and failures it exposes, the potential it holds for deconstructing the dominant idea of Quebec's homogenous Frenchness. There are knots in our shared experiences and intimate lives that can be used to complicate our understandings of the world; they can sensitize us to the fact that political imaginaries are constructed. In the plasticity, contradictoriness, and subtlety of political imaginaries, people find their awkward, unvarnished ways of existing, without the need to negate the Other.

The political forces in this horizontal experience of situated lives have been smothered to a certain extent, but they also have been mobilized and resignified by the Québécois political grand trunk railway, beginning with Louis-Joseph Papineau, the *patriote* exiled from 1837 to 1838, and running right up to René Lévesque, the failed democrat of 1980. This classic (and elitist) reading

of Quebec has sometimes greedily insisted on defining Quebec, violently prohibiting any questioning of its image. It is a reading that has inhibited the very
material and symbolic forces that could set in motion a political thought stemming from francophone colonial experience on this continent. Today, as a result, it feeds an immobilized, inhospitable posture.

I wager that there is a decolonial thought to be decoded in the muddy indeterminacy of subaltern speech, even if we must read against the grain,
bring a certain amount of irony, and assume certain hysterias and melan-
cholias. In this approach, subaltern speech is not simply what people say, it
is also what they do, what they live; it refers to the traces and materials of
popular memory. Subaltern speech is the living process in which our speaking and doing are inseparable.[4]

In the spirit of an auto-history of the place from which I am born, below
I undertake an indiscriminate excavation of the subaltern francophone imaginary. I attempt to trace the outlines of a subversive view within the national
Québécois narrative, not for the sake of an alternative vision of Canada but
in order to expose the minor sediments of living culture, situated here: the
imperial foundation, in found fragments. This in order to experiment, to open
understanding to what exists independently of what I wish to find.

Frontier Town, New York

In my aunt's shed, I found a collection of slides documenting the life of my
maternal family line from the beginning of the 1960s to the first half of the
1980s, collected and preserved for who knows what purpose. Birthdays, religious holidays, summer holidays, family reunions, fishing trips, and special
occasions (baptisms, marriages): the essential moments my grandfather chose
to capture with his amateur camera, an Ansco Rokkor 45mm. The slides were
stored in carousels and periodically projected at family gatherings. As a child,
I participated in these ceremonies of family remembrance held in my grandmother's living room, a room reserved for visiting and holidays.

All of this took place in Lévis, across the river from Quebec City – where
I grew up, where my parents and grandparents were born into families who
lived from the river, in the maritime blue-collar quarters on either side of the

Saint Lawrence: the Labadie district, Bienville, the suburb of Caron, Anse-au-Foulon, New Liverpool (also called Charny), and before then, in the eighteenth and nineteenth centuries, in the *seigneuries* of Côte-de-Beaupré, Beauport, Sainte-Foy, Île d'Orléans, and the Côte-du-Sud. A world of workers, artisans, hosteliers, boatmen, *habitants*, housewives; crocheted curtains, visits by the priest, marriages, baptisms, and burials. A world of poliomyelitis, tuberculosis, drownings, Chaudière River fishing adventures, swimming on the south shore, wild strawberries and raspberries in summertime, games along the railway line, caves in the headlands, churches, cemetaries, and plaster Virgin Marys. After longstanding summertime cohabitation with several thousand Abenaki, Maliseet, Mi'gmaq, and other citizens of the Indigenous world in the nineteenth century, Lévis, on the right bank of the river between Saint-Nicolas and Saint-Michel, was essentially a white world in the early twentieth century. It was a francophone world in which only the working men heard the bosses' English, a world of songs, radio and television, large families, American cousins; a world in which contact with other cultures was rare and education was neither important nor reasonable. Nevertheless, it was a world of socio-economic aspirations: renters, workers hired by the week, eaters of trout and partridge – people of my grandparents' generation sought to get out of what they saw as their poverty. They wanted new houses, cars, Florida, family vacations.

Family archives can be the source of what Walter Benjamin called dialectical images.[5] These tightly bound, prickly knots of time and space have a dual character: history replays itself in them and yet, at the same time, the knots surface at exactly those points where history is blocked, derailed, or folded onto itself. They thus offer a privileged research site for the exercise of critically reflexive nostalgia, a potential route to something like a non-productivist disaffiliation from colonial thought. The substance of freedom for the paupers of settler colonialism, their humble contribution to decolonial history, may lie in this nonproductive disaffiliation, which involves affective and therapeutic labour. It consists in navigating the partial excavations of worlds crumpled in upon themselves, migrating while staying in place, refusing to identify with the project of continued colonialism, learning to abandon the state.

As I revisited the photographic corpus created by my grandfather, accustomizing myself to the meticulous and repetitive labour of numbering every

Figure 4.1
A trip to Frontier Town, North Hudson, New York, 1962.

single slide, one particular series attracted my attention. It documents a family trip to the American Appalachians at the beginning of the 1960s. Some of the pictures focus on a visit to a theme park for tourists. Frontier Town, with its typical streets of high-fronted shops, its train, horses, "cowboys and Indians," and pillory, was a choice tourist destination from the 1950s to the 1970s. It offered a version of the Wild West show, with a rodeo and skill-testing games, and Indigenous actors in pow-wow regalia performing the songs, drumming, and hoop dancing of the cultures of the southwest.[6] My uncle can be seen in one of the photos. He is a child, about five years old, posing in front of an audience of tourists with one of the Indigenous actors. Docile, held in the tender gaze of his mother who stands in the far right of the frame, he holds a toy handgun.

The family vacation was a moment of exception in the life of a French Canadian family of this era. All the more so because one took the route to "the States," the seat of a whole continental imaginary for the children of my parents' generation and particularly for the boys, who played "cowboys and Indians," mimicking the films of the period. In this cardboard village in the Adirondacks, at the north end of New York State, reality and fiction are confused as a little boy from Lévis meets a "real Indian" from the United States. It is an intercultural meeting, overdetermined by colonial frames. Each is enjoined to play a role: the brown man bows with a gracefulness that seems to cite colonial fantasy; the white man – here, a little boy – holds the gun.

As Seen on TV[7]

My maternal grandfather repaired and sold radios and televisions, beginning in the 1950s. In his own way, he contributed to the great electrification of Canado-Québécois speech that powered the creation of modern Quebec, the Quebec of "masters in our own house." It was on television that Georges Dor sang "La Manic" to us.[8] And, one might say, it was with the arrival of television in French Canadian homes in the 1950s that a new form of anti-Indigenous racism was disseminated. The advent of television, at the very least, accelerated and crystallized the hold of the North American colonial imaginary, through the genre of the Western.

The Innu writer and knowledge keeper An Antane Kapesh[9] is unequivocal about the influence of filmic imagery on white (and especially, Québécois) perceptions of Indigenous peoples. Focusing on the context of Quebec, she argues that in the 1970s this filmic image corresponded to a colonial imaginary, not the realities of Indigenous peoples:

Now that we live the White man's life, we often meet journalists and filmmakers. When we lived our Innu life inland, we never saw them. I consider that today, when we are talked about in the newspapers, there is nothing true there, and when you see us in films or on television, there is nothing true there.

Because nowadays, it is not our own life that we are living. Me, an Innu woman, I find this life that we live now, which is the White man's, tiresome and harmful; I find my life is very different since I have been living according to White culture. The only reason why I am happy to meet journalists and filmmakers today is to show the White man that he did not bring us up well. As an Innu woman, this is the only reason that I agree to be seen on television and in films, but there is nothing real in that. And I am not uncomfortable to appear in films because I know that had I lived the way the Innu used to in the past, today I would never have been seen in films or on television and no one would have talked about me in the newspapers.[10]

In essence she writes, if I were myself, if I were not colonized, no one would see me on television. This is why she feels no self-consciousness before the camera: it is not her that we see, but rather what the settler-colonial imaginary has made of Indigenous peoples. The television version of Indigeneity is a colonial spectre: "there is nothing real in that."

The role of the sound-image in the development of anti-Indigenous racism in Quebec is equally apparent in the discrepancy between the two protagonists in the celebrated 1963 documentary *Pour la suite du monde*, by Pierre Perrault:[11] between Alexis Tremblay, who was already an elderly man when the film was made, and his son, Léopold, who was in the prime of his youth. When it comes to explaining the source of the beluga whale-hunting technique used by the people of the Île-aux-Coudres, 150 kilometres east of Lévis, a technique in the process of being recovered in the period during which the film was being made, Tremblay, the father, and his friend Louis Harvey, are clear: it was the "savages" who invented this practice, and the "savage," for these elderly men, is a "genius." The statement is repeated almost as a jingle in the course of the film. The son, Léopold, vehemently refuses the attribution, suggesting that it must be false... since it is impossible. He buttresses his view by calling on the stereotypes of the primitive or lazy Indigenous person, figures he supposes provide proof of a lack of genius.[12]

The exasperated father, having furnished his son with solid arguments in support of his thesis, exclaims: "You are a controversialist! If you don't believe what the ancestors have passed down to us..." The son, Léopold, has no arguments to support his conviction regarding a French origin for the beluga whale hunt. He has only a mental blockage, a desire for debate, which surfaces as soon as the possibility of inheriting knowledge from Indigenous peoples is placed before him. He is a cheater, envious, having lost his hunting heritage. In this scene about the passing on of tradition, he plays his proper role for Perrault's camera. Léopold is a bit of a buccaneer; he has the spirit of a plunderer: hunting cannot *not* be French, even if there is no evidence to support his view. Hunting is "ours," and we are not "them."

On the sources of a colonial imaginary in *Canadian* culture, Daniel Francis, born in 1947, writes:

I learned how to play Indian from movies and television. But where did children of an earlier generation learn? There were books of course, novels of juvenile adventures set in the northern woods and the great western plains, written by missionaries and hacks with as much knowledge of aboriginal people as they had of the people from the remotest Africa. There was school, where young students absorbed the history of their country, including stories of the role played by Indians. Before World War I, there was the Wild West Show, where city youngsters got an exciting taste of cowboys and Indians. And in the early years of the twentieth century, there was a remarkable youth movement which took its inspiration from the image of the Noble Indian and tried to introduce children to the pleasure and values of wilderness life. All these Indians – the Indians of fiction, of the Wild West Show, of schoolbooks and summer camps – were imaginary.[13]

In the 1950s, North American popular culture, in Quebec as elsewhere, disseminated the colonial fantasy of the Western. The fantasy was constructed at the end of the nineteenth century through spectacles like Frontier Town, school textbooks (in Quebec, put together by religious communities dedicated to children's education), and the culture promoted by various outdoor recreation organizations (notably, in Quebec, the Boy Scouts Association of Canada).[14] Léopold, the character in Perrault's documentary, is a product of the arrival of television in French Canadian homes. It is through television that he inherits the North American popular culture of the early twentieth century, which includes radio and pulp fiction. He is also the inheritor of a world in which cohabitation with Indigenous peoples in the history of the Saint Lawrence River valley has been completely repudiated and erased.

As for his father, Alexis (born in 1886), he draws on a work that deals with the *habitant* traditions of the Île-aux-Coudres, including quotation from the journal of Jacques Cartier on the subject of the beluga whale hunt. He reads out an extract for the patriarchs who are assembled in the village's blacksmith shop, addressing his son, Léopold, in particular. He cites what he sees as the direct testimony of Cartier, as well as the island's oral tradition, which is for

Alexis a straight-from-the-horse's-mouth source of precisely those facts needed in the dispute between the island's generations. The testimony is clearly a representation, but it is a representation that contains elements of technique as well as general description; it has an air of plausibility, with regard to both the historical experience of the beluga whale hunt and the account of its transmission as knowledge.

On the basis of this inherited knowledge, Alexis is in a position to bear indirect witness to the lives of Indigenous beluga whale hunters on the river, drawing from Cartier's narrative but also from the oral tradition of the islanders. As An Antane Kapesh writes, the way of life she has known and lived is not seen on television. Alexis' insistence on an Indigenous source of knowledge, impossible to his son, resonates with her point.

The son is resolutely on the other side of the screen; he has been raised within the society of the spectacle.[15] This society admits only those phantasmagoric "savages" who, Léopold gathers from the evidence of the screen, would be incapable of inventing a technique of beluga whale hunting. The beluga whale caught in the course of the filming of Pour la suite du monde was triumphantly delivered to a New York aquarium by Léopold. In the end, the whale, like everyone else, including my five-year-old uncle holding his little gun, plays a prescribed role within the colonial spectacle.

Children's Tales

Boys of my age, in the 1980s, were, like their fathers and uncles, lovingly outfitted as cowboys by their mothers. The stories that served as the settings for their games involved fights between cowboys and Indians, even though they did not quite know why, since the days of the Western had long since passed. In fact, this was the era in which Frontier Town would close its doors for lack of interest on the part of tourists.[16]

Of course, "cowboys and Indians" are figures of fantasy; they are the figures of a colonial imaginary. The banal products of a continuously replaying colonial-kitsch aesthetic, they are a cultural component of the material and symbolic capture upholding the state form in America.[17] In the colonial scene, one might say, each one of us is a construct, a character, as in a video game or a pornographic film: we are fully engaged in our roles, heart and soul, but

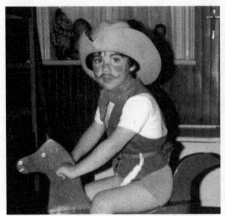 

Figures 4.2 and 4.3
A little Catholic cowboy, and children festooned with feathers.

what we are engaged in is not reality. Colonialism operates on the line between reality and fiction, in the muddy common sense[18] (or *epistemic murk*) through which violence gets overwritten by fiction, obfuscated, reported, fantasized, rendered fluid and spectacular.

I wrote to my aunt, the eldest in the family, in order to ask about the photographs of Frontier Town and what she could tell me about this family trip. She replied:

It's a very good memory. A trip to the States with C— and M— who were not yet married at that time. We set out in the big Meteor, four adults and four children. It was 1962, I think; M— was a baby. The photo is from a completely fake Far West village, with cowboys and Indians. I was about eleven and I adored that stuff; I hadn't yet learned irony and cynicism. We bought ourselves jeans and red gingham shirts, the epitome of sophistication.

With some further research I was able to establish that the man posing with my uncle was named Swift Eagle.[19] He was an Indigenous performer and presenter from New Mexico. He lived and worked in Frontier Town, along with his wife, Chee Chee Bird, and their children (Singing Eagle, Dancing Eagle [Dany], Powhatan, and Matoaka), between 1954 and 1968. His daughter, Matoaka Little Eagle, who is still living, has described the Frontier Town era and its political ambiance. I include one of her accounts here:

> I am so glad that my father, Swift Eagle, was strong and committed to be himself, as a Native man, with respect and integrity. I felt bad for my oldest brother because when we first stared working there, the management convinced him to be an Indian that scared passengers on the stagecoach by messing up their hair. Poor guy would come home with bruises and marks on his body. Besides that, it was demeaning and just [perpetuated] a one-sided biased history of the west that did not look upon the actual history with enough references to what was happening with Native people at the time … Understand that in the 1950s, it was very difficult to be a Native person, in real life, and to have people mock you, disrespect you, and even physically hurt you. It is not so easy to understand that they are playing and living their fantasies, while you are living your life. There is a clash of reality and surrealism. When people do not want to believe that you are really what you say you are, and continue to disrespect you, it goes to racism, not fun. It took me many years to understand that many people were just ignorant of actual history or they had been educated to believe that manifest destiny was ok and justified the taking of land and the massacre of thousands of Native people – real men, women, and children, my relations. They also learned a lot of stereotypes and misinformation from school, movies, and tv. I'm not trying to lay a guilt trip on anyone. I'm just saying that there was a lot more happening at Frontier Town than what people saw on the surface. It took a lot of work for me to just be a little Indian girl who wanted to play and make friends, when people would hit me with their stereotype comments and refuse to see the real me.[20]

As Matoaka Little Eagle writes, it is not easy to understand that while white children amused themselves in a fantasy universe of "cowboys and Indians," Indigenous peoples were simply living their lives. They were living real life, but within a universe that made their lives into a colonial fantasy. Matoaka's family members were necessarily aware of the fact that it was a colonial representation that people attacked with their comments; it was a fantasy, but it was one that denied their humanity.

An Antane Kapesh, in her *I Am a Damn Savage, Eukuan nin matshi-manitu innushkueu*, takes us to the other side of such a colonial façade, as she tells of her experience of Schefferville's centenary celebrations of the discovery of iron ore in the region. According to the settler narrative retailed by the three-day long celebration, the ore mine was discovered thanks to Schefferville's white fathers (an erroneous attribution, according to the oral tradition known by Kapesh). Innu were asked to lend themselves to the staging of this discovery, playing their "proper" role, in traditional dress, and preparing a feast beneath the *shaputuan*. Some also were asked to perform as missionary-discoverers, in full missionary robes. This reconstruction of the founding scene of the Québécois Côte-Nord was also the occasion for a visit by the then prime minister of Canada, Pierre Trudeau. Kapesh astutely underlines the authoritarian nature of this conjunction of the lie of discovery with the visit of the head of state: "On the first day, Trudeau came to see the festivities because it was at that moment that the untold story of who discovered iron ore, that is, Father Babel, here in the North, would be revealed."[21]

The Ojibwe theorist Gail Valaskakis helps us to understand the politics of this gap between Indigenous reality and its folklorized colonial image, the gap of which An Antane Kapesh and Matoaka Little Eagle write. Valaskakis shows how dominant representations do violence to real Indigenous presence in America.

This distinction between Native North American heritage and "real" history situates Indians "outside history," where they can be erased, displaced, reified, and named. The vanquished have been drawn in the words of the victors, whose assertion that oral tradition is folklore, not history, constructs Indians as historyless vagrants without an authenticated written past. Like ethnographic constructions, these competing conceptions of history and folklore are linked to representations that reinforce the dominant culture's understanding of the Indian as noble or evil, villainous or victimized. Drawn from the images of the romanticized or savage Indian, neither representation allows newcomers to identify

Native peoples as equals, or to recognize Native North Americans as "real inhabitants of the land" … The history that assigns these images to Indians also constructs the nation-states they inhabit, creating an imagined coherence and commonness among newcomers that excludes Native people.[22]

The gap between Indigenous reality and dominant colonial imagery, as the daughter of Swift Eagle tells us, produces white children's "refus[al] to see the real Matoaka." It prevents settlers from thinking about the Indigenous person as an equal and permits continued territorial expulsion. Gerald Vizenor names this settler cultural trait "manifest manners" (referring to the doctrine of manifest destiny mentioned by Matoaka Little Eagle) and describes it as consisting in the "courses of dominance, the racialist notions and misnomers sustained in archives and lexicon as 'authentic' representations of Indian cultures. Manifest manners court the destiny of monotheism, cultural determinism, objectivism, and the structural conceits of savagism and civilization."[23] These "manners" are enacted in North Hudson, New York, as in Schefferville, Quebec – Western scenes staged to provide entertainment for the children, employment for those whose cultures are supposedly fading, and an infinite reproduction of the theatre of settler colonialism.

The colonial fantasy of the Western had its heyday in Quebec in the 1960s. Performers like those at Frontier Town, working according to the model of the Wild West show, appeared in different towns of the northeast. They also appeared in Montreal stage shows, in commercial venues. In 1967, on the occasion of the celebration of Canada's centenary, they appeared in a Montreal parade. In some archival images, one can see Frontier Town performers on horseback, accompanied by French Canadian rivals, celebrity cowboys wearing fleur-de-lys flags: Willie Lamothe, the Western icon,[24] Frenchie Jarraud, inventor of Quebec talk show radio, and Jean Drapeau, the mayor of Montreal who outfitted himself as a cowboy for official occasions. Montreal was another Frontier Town.

As for the little boy with the gun in the photo taken at Frontier Town by my grandfather, the television repairman: at the end of his adolescence, my uncle enlisted with the Canadian Armed Forces and participated in the Canadian peacekeeping mission in Cyprus. The objective was to hold apart

Figure 4.4
Jean Drapeau, mayor of Montreal, greets Frontier Town performers.

Greek and Turkish forces on the island, helping to seal the border between the "Orient" and the "West." He quit the army as soon as his enlistment contract allowed.

• • •

The great secularist cowboys of today are the descendants of the little Catholic cowboys of yesterday. They carry inherited suspicions and antipathies, "Without knowing or wanting to know or being able to know" (Hector de Saint-Denys Garneau),[25] that is, without knowing why or in the name of what fear they hold to these things. Deprived of any concrete fraternity with the Indigenous world, they reproduce the stereotypes that make anti-Indigenous racism ordinary in Quebec. "A certain kind of work was never done," as Rémi Savard wrote at the end of the 1970s, "and from this failure issues a secularism that is incapable of speaking of Indigenous peoples without either assimilating them or folklorizing them."[26] The unresolved psychopolitics of European arrival in America persist in deep layers of the collective consciousness, alongside the contemporary structural racism and the anti-immigrant sentiment galloping across Quebec. A certain kind of work was never done...

5

The Paupers of Settler Colonialism

It is difficult to innovate in a province that has not revolutionized its fantasmatic relation to authority, to its neobiblical discourse, a province that has not liberated itself from the tutelage of its multiple metropoles and profits from "true wisdom" while economizing on the stormy and creative historical process.

Robert Hébert[1]

I occasionally return to a conversation that was one of those transformative moments in which, suddenly, a whole field of action came into view for me. It was at the end of the 2000s, on the University of Ottawa campus. Georges E. Sioui[2] and I were seated in an old student café called the Nostalgica; the café would be flattened shortly thereafter, to make way for a new, modern structure (you can't make this stuff up). Georges had been at the Institute of Canadian Studies (today, the Institute of Indigenous Research and Studies at the University of Ottawa) since 2004, heading a new program of Indigenous Studies. I was in the early years of a very assiduous reading of contemporary Indigenous literature and political thought. I was intensely engaged in thinking about how to form alliances with Indigenous struggles and how to contribute to the visibility of the global Indigenous resurgence, which has been called the Indigenous renaissance since the 1960s.[3]

Nostalgia on the Circle's Outer Edge

In that era, I was sometimes teaching this Indigenous literature alongside Indigenous political issues, in a context that was very different from the one we know today. The program for Indigenous Studies, with which I periodically associated myself, ran on very few resources. Those in positions of power at the university – the majority of them white men, anglophones and franco-phones – saw Indigenous Studies from on high. From their point of view, it was a marginal subject, if not a fad, of doubtful value and seriousness. In-digenous contributions to philosophy, history, and literature were almost completely absent from the university curriculum and Indigenous episte-mologies were simply beneath the radar. Only a small minority worked on these questions within the university. It was the era in which the United Na-tions Declaration on the Rights of Indigenous Peoples (UNDRIP) was being drafted, well before its eventual adoption by Canada. It was before the Gov-ernment of Canada apology for residential schools, before the Truth and Rec-onciliation Commission (TRC), before the National Inquiry into Missing and Murdered Indigenous Women and Girls, before the Viens Commission,[4] and before the generalization of the practice of territorial acknowledgement. It was before the current era of "reconciliation," still to deliver on its promises, as the recent large demonstrations in support of the hereditary Wet'suwet'en chiefs show us.[5]

Georges' arrival on campus was a huge event. The first Indigenous person to obtain a doctorate in history in Canada, he had already published two major works, translated into several languages: *For an Amerindian Autohistory: An Essay on the Foundations of a Social Ethic*, first published in 1989, and *Huron-Wendat: The Heritage of the Circle*, in 1994.[6] I would be involved in the prepa-ration of his third book, a collection of essays and speeches entitled *Histoires de Kanatha/Histories of Kanatha*, which was published in 2009.[7] Georges brought something new to the university, something he termed a "circular vi-sion of the world." This vision brought with it a practice of respecting all be-ings, as well as a remarkable oral artistry that defied all of the university's codes of *habitus*.[8] He was on a mission to introduce all who were interested to the ways of the First Peoples, in the most open and inclusive way. For Georges, everyone could accede to this way of thinking and seeing. Alliance was inherent to his thought; he admitted of no hierarchy between living be-ings. His hospitality was absolute. He believed that each of us had a right to the bounty of nature.

Georges also had a revolutionary approach to the history of the Americas, which he called auto-history. Picking up on Vine Deloria Jr.'s idea of a return to Indigenous science,[9] Georges articulated an approach to history that put the colonial archive in conversation with the oral tradition. This approach seeks not to refute the discipline of history as it has been constituted in Western modernity, but rather to reframe the colonial archive, whether it is the *Jesuit Relations*, European explorers' narratives, or ceremonial artefacts preserved in museums, in the interest of an Indigenous history of America grounded in contemporary Indigenous thought.[10] For Georges, this thought inherits a whole tradition of place-based thinking and it speaks from a circular cosmology. In this way of thinking about history, ethics takes the place of chronology, and an attentiveness to relationality takes the place of the accumulation of facts.

The history of the Americas told through an Indigenous onto-epistemology is at the heart of the panamerican approach I was encountering, with some trepidation, in my reading in the 2000s:

The Mi'gmaw poet Rita Joe
The Mi'gmaw historian Daniel N. Paul
The Innu writer An Antane Kapesh
The Anishinaabeg elder and social worker Herb Nabigon
The Haudenosaunee legal scholar Patricia Monture-Angus
The Mohawk political philosopher Taiaiake Alfred
The Seneca historian John Mohawk
The Ojibwe linguist and storyteller Basil H. Johnston
The Ojibwe literary theorist Gerald Vizenor
The Ojibwe cultural critic Gail Guthrie Valaskakis
The Ojibwe legal scholar and philosopher John Borrows
The Ojibwe writer Louise Erdrich
The Menominee writer and activist Chrystos
The Cree poet Louise Bernice Halfe
The Cree writer, lawyer, and activist Harold Cardinal
The Cree writer Tomson Highway
The Cree theatre director and playwright Floyd Favel
The Métis elder and writer Maria Campbell
The Métis writer Beatrice Culleton Mosionier
The Métis activist Howard Adams
The Cree and Métis historian Olive P. Dickason

The Métis literary critic Emma LaRocque
The Sto:lo writer Lee Maracle
The Syilx writer Jeannette Armstrong
The Laguna-Sioux poet and literary critic Paula Gunn Allen
The Osage literary and cultural critic Robert Allen Warrior
The Kiowa and Cherokee writer N. Scott Momaday
The Cherokee novelist Thomas King

And there were others, too, a fierce generation of Indigenous renaissance writers and theorists, the memory of which is too easily effaced, it seems to me, in the presentist era of reconciliation.

Seated with Georges in the Nostalgica, I explained how I felt myself to be in a difficult political position, as a white Québécoise of colonial ancestry in America, a position I was obliged to acknowledge in the face of the Indigenous world's ethical injunction to speak the truth of who we are and take up the responsibilities that stem from our historical positioning. I told him in the most candid way, about this thing that it costs me to expose, and yet, it is this very costliness that tells me: this is exactly what must be done.

I said to Georges: In the struggle against colonialism, Indigenous peoples can seize their roots, their millennial history, their living traditions, which carry a memory of liberty and equality. You have the power of a civilization that is not empire; you have a tangible, concrete imaginary that can oppose itself to a world in the thrall of hierarchy and extractivism. For my part, I told him, I look behind me, I rifle through the past, and I find nothing that can catalyse me: neither a native heritage that would constitute a *codex* of liberty in this territory, nor a European heritage that could guide me toward a relation to the land other than commodification, expropriation, extraction, accumulation, diversion. The inheritance I need I do not have; the inheritance I have, I do not want. When one issues from the Quebec-that-is-descended-from-France and one turns to the past in search of a way of living together, a way of situating oneself so as to contest actually-existing Canada, what one finds before and beneath colonialism is another colonialism, like a set of Russian dolls. Before the British Empire and the Dominion of Canada, there was New France, another colonial regime, which is the cause, if not the origin, of francophone America. In the end, I don't know why I am here, I told him.

Georges said to me: "You are realizing something important there; you must write about that one day." In essence, this condition of being without an inheritance is a chance at something. I think Georges was speaking of the opportunity of those with nothing to defend and thus perhaps of those with nothing to lose, nothing to protect. Georges, in his patient, non-judgemental way, was inviting me to see that in this feeling of cultural dispossession and political incapacity that I was sharing so awkwardly with him, there was possibility, there was a starting point. He reminded me – at least, this is how I recall his words – that one can make something of nothing, that there is force, potential, even liberty in it. There is something like a window opening onto disaffiliation, which could be the beginning of a contribution to the world of decolonizing struggles.

More than a decade after this conversation, with the confessionalism and egocentrism of that moment now sifted out (I hope), I continue to reflect on the political tenor of the affects animating colonized populations, which are part of what one could call the intimate matter of colonialism, the imperial foundations of a people's *habitus*.[11] The ambiguous sentiments, the dubious claims to being in alliance, the blundering language, even: when these are admitted and explored, critically examined and deconstructed, they can constitute the very material of decolonial mobilization. There are transversal routes in the elucidation of the things that wound the ego; in the fantasy of the disintegrating, fragile, imperilled self; in the stuff of shame. Finding these routes requires introspective work, the study of those things that irrigate culture and political life as they move through people, beyond their conscience and their will; it requires excavation of the affective materials that constitute and sustain racial categories, exclusions, symbolic violence. The work must be undertaken without omitting oneself from these dynamics, and while fully acknowledging that one's language is situated in space and time.[12]

At the time of this conversation with my Wendat colleague at the Nostalgica in 2009, I was expressing through osmosis, without knowing it, the sense of cultural impoverishment that constitutes a nationalist trauma for many Québécois: the sense of finding oneself in "my grandfather's boat in this illiterate darkness," in the words of Gaston Miron."[13] The sense of disinheritance can take different forms, but notably expresses itself in colonial nostalgia, where one is inhabited by the memory of something missing, something lacking, the absence of which causes us suffering but which we are incapable of mourning since it is something we have never known. Nostalgia is the mourning of an absence, a painful hollow that points to a space where something precious should be, to what should have been there. One's psyche refuses to separate itself from this feeling that replaces the missing thing, and holds one captive.

Psychopathology of Keb[14]

In this admission of colonial disinheritance, and in this inability to mourn – to mourn the very idea that there is something to mourn – one finds a source of envy. Lacking European identity, or not being European enough while not really being anything else; lacking a great culture, and existing as a kind of branch plant of France in America; lacking a language that proclaims itself a window onto the whole world, and speaking a minor colonial idiom, what one really longs for, as a settler descended from settlers, without admitting it, is to be Indigenous, to be like Indigenous peoples, to be able to reclaim something belonging to ourselves, a millennial rooting. One longs to be able to inherit a struggle, a freedom, a decolonial futurity, a political position proper to (what is for us) the New World. One longs to exist politically, and on solid, real, noble ground.

Settlers, those inheritors of violence and usurpation, who assume the duty and task of dominating a world they neither know nor wish to know, long to take the place of the colonized. They long to take this place in order to fill a constitutive sense of lack, in order to be able to cease suffering, at their own hands, from a derisory cause, their sensed lack of collective existence.[15] They envy what they see as the colonized's sense of being at home in the world, of having a place in it. Not just the lengthy continuity of that place, but its legitimacy, its mythology, its feats.

In this sense, because of this envy and bad faith, the nostalgic settler seems very close to the figure of the *mauvais pauvre* in the poetry of Hector de Saint-Denys Garneau, which the critic Yvon Rivard identifies as an archetype for the Québécois writer:

> The *mauvais pauvre*, in sum, is the one who impedes the wheels of progress, the one "who prowls around your riches and breaks-and-enters

into your happiness." You can try to give him money, joy, certainty, memories, ideals, but he cannot retain anything, "there is a hole in him
through which everything escapes." The more you give him, the poorer
he is, his poverty grows in proportion to all the riches he has not been
able to keep, and that is why, says Saint-Denys Garneau, "He is irre-
deemably poor." He is so poor that he does not even have memories![16]

The Québécois pauper, if we take Garneau himself as an example, is a little
white Catholic, an inferior from the point of view French culture, who nevertheless claims to descend from a line of noblemen or titled landowners. He
participates in the world of letters, he is not illiterate; he has been educated.
He lives between Westmount in Montreal, the cultural and economic
metropolis, and Sainte-Catherine-de-Fossambault, the former *seigneury*.

But the other side of the equation, the other side of the pauper's obsession
with Europe's view of America as nothing but a mark of his own impoverishment, is something that usually stays hidden and yet is an essential part of
the "identitarian" equation. The pauper is all of the above things, but he is
also on unceded Indigenous land. The *Canadien francais*-become-Québécois,
if I may be permitted this extrapolation from Rivard's analysis, benefits from
everything possible in this Indigenous land, which he has occupied con-
sciously or unconsciously, passively or actively. He has been given everything:
money, joy, certainty, memories, ideals. And yet, nothing sticks; everything
escapes him. He is unhappy. He is incapable of receiving the hospitality extended to him, he clings to the idea of his poverty, to his taste for being in the
position of the Other (in relation to the Indigenous as well as to Europe), to
his self-loathing. Handicapped by this feeling, he is the *mauvais pauvre*, the
"irredeemable" pauper,[17] according to Garneau's apt phrase. But there is more.
Rivard asks:

But why would this sort of infirmity with which he is afflicted make him
not just poor, but a pauper? Why doesn't this extreme destitution enlist
our deepest feelings of compassion? Why couldn't we grant him the status of being, simply, poor, not just in order to clear our conscience but
to thank him for assuming the poverty that is the cost of any wealth?
Because "he is poor and therefore a stranger, in other words, he has nothing, nothing to exchange. But he's not playing straight, he wants in."[18]

The Québécois pauper is wretched because he clings to his poverty, to the source of his suffering, to his inferiority, and at the same time, he will not accept that he has nothing to exchange: he *wants in*. It is his envy that manifests itself here, his gaze from below, and this is what makes him dangerous. He is dishonest – with himself, most importantly. Sensing that he is inferior, the "Keb" is obsessed with his own impostor status. He benefits from all the modern comforts – from education, health care, Confederation, citizenship, cultural dominance, territorial domination – and yet he is still an inferior in relation to Europe, French culture, the English of the British regime for whom he will never be more than a little master. He is inferior, too, in relation to the immigrant who seems to him to have more of a right to difference, a less tortured relation to his culture. And he is inferior in relation to the Indigenous, who have access to the political legitimacy of the colonized in the face of empire, as well as a link to the land. He knows he lacks something and he identifies with this lack, claiming it, even though it has never existed. His is the colonial nostalgia affecting Québécois national thought – the expression of a bottomless poverty, a mental wound caused by a fraudulence, sensed but deeply denied.

The Québécois pauper is here for no reason, or for the wrong reasons, and prefers to die rather than admit it – in fact, prefers to kill. Traditional Quebec is the pauper of British settler colonialism in North America: what it wants is to be colonized, to be the *only* one colonized, the better to accede to the position of master.

Of Wealth and Poverty in America

Georges E. Sioui evokes the figure of poverty as he reflects on the foundations of the colonial relation from his own, Wendat, perspective. He writes with compassion of a Europe that was deeply sickened and impoverished at the moment of contact in the fifteenth century, having arrived in a richly abundant America only through wandering, accident, and misfortune.

Europe itself, in the moment of its accidental arrival in America, was but a great foyer for epidemics, such was the extent of the Circle's replacement with the Line. This chronically and mortally ill Europe, it might even be said, was searching frenetically for a remedy and a salvation at the end of the fifteenth century.[19]

Europe's sickness, according to Sioui, is a physical and cultural one, characterized by its replacement of the Circle, the cosmology of ancient peoples, with the Line, a civilization of expropriation, extraction, accumulation, and destruction. He suggests that for the descendants of the original colonizers, the only possible (decolonial) interpretation of the encounter of Europe and America, the only source of a reason for being here, is the idea that Europe came to America for the purpose of collective, cultural healing, in order to remake the foundations of its civilization.

Thus, the only acceptable reason for celebrating the arrival of Europeans here in 1492 would be the physical salvation of a Europe that had been condemned to death, and its gradual return to physical, mental, and spiritual well-being, in the healthy and wholesome air of the amerindian Great Island. This project of healing, still incomplete, is something to which Amerindians continue to wish to contribute. For those of us whose hearts beat with the rhythm of this America, this land giving life to all, this is what we reflect upon, while other hearts still celebrate an old, abandoned world that promised nothing but death.[20]

The figure of the envious pauper, incapable of rising out of the poverty to which he clings, the pauper who wishes to be wealthy but is incapable of becoming so through his own means, may be seen as the sulky inheritor of the sick European in search of an American remedy. The pauper's meanness, his sense of cultural inferiority, perhaps stems from the European's belief in the superiority of his own, gangrenous civilization – which has much work to do in order to heal itself, since it still must learn how to distinguish between what heals and what kills. This dimension of the Québécois psyche is evident to Pierrot Ross-Tremblay, who uses the image of a cultural disease for his articulation of an Innu perspective on settler colonialism in the Saint Lawrence River valley:

Such a society is overwhelmed by a cultural scorbus that makes it desire the symbolic vitamins of millennial cultures that, paradoxically, it cannot help but invisibilize. The society imposed on Innu people has not only a strong propensity to forget, but a reprehensible drive to erase what preceded it in order to perceive itself as "sovereign." Yet the small mirror explorers gave in exchange for a territory that cannot be "owned" would come to haunt their descendants. Simulated blindness and deafness have their limits. Self-ignorance and denial do not, in fact, change the nature of the relationship between the Innu and settler population of Quebec. The identification of Quebec nationalists as a colonized people has weak foundations.[21]

What the settler-pauper envies, even as he denies its value, is a particular kind of wealth, a condition of health that belongs to the civilization of the Circle. The pauper insists that he is the only possible source of wealth, and yet, his hands are empty. He cannot stand for his poverty to be exposed and so the Other who sees his empty hands must be made to disappear. Even better (and even more cowardly, on the part of the one who wishes for this), the Other should be made like him, should be made to desire to be him, since this would confirm his place and value in America, precisely through the destruction of any competing values. As a man who was a pauper of this kind asserted to me, quite unabashedly, after hearing me present on this theme: "Personally, I like colonialism; if there hadn't been colonialism, I wouldn't be here!" Rosa Pires provides a similar illustration of this phenomenon, paraphrasing a response to her study of second-generation immigrant women's voices:

> At the end of the day, and saying it straight, it is the immigrants who don't try hard enough to integrate. "We" of Québec, "we" have some things to correct, but we're extraordinary! My history is extraordinary and everyone should ground themselves in my history in order to become like me! And when you don't make the effort to take the hand of those who are offering you hospitality, well, that's pushing it, you don't deserve to be here.[22]

• • •

Sioui grew up in Wendake,[23] in the northwest of Quebec City, in the heart of the Catholic-cowboy universe of Quebec in the 1950s and 1960s. As a child, from my bedroom window, which had also been that of my mother, her sisters, and her brother, I could see, on the other side of the river, the mouth of the Saint Charles River that led to what we called the Hurons' Village, in the period. In the 1980s, when Sioui studied at Laval University (like me, just a few years later) and wrote *For an Amerindian Autohistory*, he moved into hostile territory, to say the least. His message would be so difficult for the paupers, the Québécois, to hear that it risked complete inaudibility. Sioui was conveying a firm intellectual and political program, founded in an entire heritage, and it was only through his own profound generosity that he managed to partially protect himself from the scorn with which his ideas were greeted (in a reception I myself would witness).

In 2005, as a young professor, I found myself along with several colleagues heading a committee to organize the annual congress of Québécois political scientists in Ottawa. The theme was to be "Territories of America," and the plenary speakers were Michel Freitag, the late Québécois sociologist (of Swiss origin); the American science fiction writer Norman Spinrad; and Sioui, the Huron-Wendat historian.[24] This transborder panel subtly skewered the modern, statist, national consensus of Québécois political science (only in order to be met with a generalized indifference, no doubt!). The choice of panelists provoked some bad press among certain colleagues in the field who saw in it an eccentricity of doubtful value. One of them exclaimed to me: "Georges E. Sioui, isn't that a bit Pocahontas?"[25]

Americity

Sioui's *For an Amerindian Autohistory* was the first Indigenous-authored book I ever read. It was at the end of my undergraduate studies in political science at Laval University, a decade before I met Sioui at the University of Ottawa. A friend who was impassioned by the Zapatista struggle in Chiapas, which was then tearing up the political sky of the Americas, loaned me a copy, thinking the argument would interest me. This was also four years after the events surrounding the so-called Oka Crisis,[26] which I had encountered through the filter of dominant Québécois representations, without really questioning them: images of Lasagne, of Warriors, and of blockaded bridges in the distant metropolis.

The book turned my world upside down. Sioui's work provided my first access to the experience of the reverse-gaze found in Indigenous contemporary writing. I was introduced to a whole other history of the Americas, other than the one I had learned, stemming from another kind of consciousness. I was introduced to something counter to the assumptions of progress: this was the theory of the Circle, conveying principles of mutuality and radical freedom, completely averse to the nation-statist onto-epistemology that I knew, and had believed to be all that existed.

I had the sense that there was something unprecedented being sketched out, a remarkable hospitality being extended: leaving Europe and arriving in America, there was a failure to see a system of peopled places – places named, organized, known, travelled – presenting a plurality of cosmologies and ways of living, a plurality in which every living being was invited to join a web of interdependent relations.

Rather than nations, the thinker of the Circle lives in societies that are, at the same time, independent and complementary in relation to one another. In the world of the Circle, humans are not the only ones with rights: "democracy" extends to other, non-human peoples. Trees, plants, animals, stones, land, water; spirits are also rights since they contribute to maintaining life as a whole.[27]

Today more than ever, the invitation to rethink democracy in a way that convenes not only every human society but all of the living, of which we are a part, is extremely compelling, ethically and politically. The Ojibwe legal scholar John Borrows echoes this invitation in the work he has been undertaking since the 1990s, a patient excavation of the constitutional foundations of contact between Indigenous peoples and Europeans in North America:

Reconciliation between Indigenous peoples and the Crown requires our collective reconciliation with the earth. Practices and partnerships of resurgence and reconciliation must sustain the living earth and our more-than-human relatives for future generations. This will not occur without the simultaneous resurgence of Indigenous laws, government, economies, education, relations to the living earth, ways of knowing and being, and treaty relationship.[28]

The perspective of the Circle also can be found in the recent Atikamekw First Nation Declaration of Sovereignty, still not acknowledged by Québécois society although made public in 2014:

> Our assertion of sovereignty means our occupation of Nitaskinan, and our engagement in our traditional practices and diplomatic relations with other nations on the basis of our oral traditions and wampum. Atikamekw Nehirowisiw has lived harmoniously with neighbour nations: the Innu to the east, the Eeyou in the north, the Abenaki Iriniw in the south, and the Anishinaabeg to the west. Atikamekw Nehirowisiw intends to maintain and exercise territorial governance over the whole of Nitaskinan. To that end, Atikamekw Nehirowisiw will ensure that its people are a political and economic entity to be contended with. The consent of Atikamekw Nehirowisiw will be required for any development, and any use and exploitation of resources in Nitaskinan. The sustainability of Nitaskinan resources will have to be guaranteed and traditional occupation by Atikamekw Nehirowisiw respected. At all times the actions of Atikamekw Nehirowisiw and its present and future institutions will be informed by the protection of Nitaskinan, the defense of its way of life and its aspirations.[29]

The goal of rethinking relations between peoples in the territory, with a view to ensuring the harmony and durability of these relations, is clear.

From Sioui's early works, conceived in his birthplace of Wendake, and stretching along the routes of Indigenous America, there is a weaving of political thought underway that is both millennial and new, and that multiplies and complexifies Indigenous voices. Through its growing reception, this political thought persists and insists; it activates other political imaginaries with a forcefulness that it would have been difficult to foresee, even a decade ago. Witness Indigenous resurgence theory, treaty philosophy, the increasingly vigorous alliances between Indigenous and environmentalist struggles, the radical nature of current decolonial theory, the powerful emergence of Indigenous literature in Quebec. There are echoes of Sioui's contribution to the renaissance of the theory of the Circle in this growing body of work. It includes the numerous contemporary Indigenous writers who inspired Rémi Savard in the 1970s. As the Anishinaabe scholar Aaron Mills writes:

> Colonialism isn't merely a process of newcomer settlement and Indigenous displacement; it's a mode of relationship between settler peoples, Indigenous peoples, and land in which all are harmed (albeit certainly not equally). Settler peoples harm themselves in founding their political community upon violence, which slowly destroys it from within. So long as they maintain their earth-alienated constitutional order, which treats non-humans as resources to be exploited, there is no escape from this fate, although settlers are always welcome to abandon their current constitutional project and, through treaty, root their political communities in earth.[30]

This is an invitation to move beyond a colonial culture founded in a violence that can only be overcome through an entire ontological and legal revocation. Immersed in this growing body of thought, Sioui wrote me, after reading the present essay:

> All my life, I have searched for a remedy, a "medicine," for those who from an early age I learned to see as my parents, in other words, all those of the human and more-than-human worlds ... This medicine, my dear friend, I believe myself to have described and explained better than ever before in the book which you are now reading, *Eatenonha* (our Mother-Earth). The essential message of that book is that if one can see oneself as a participant in healing, one can be delivered from the abominable, unbearable weight of feeling like a pauper, pernicious to life itself.[31]

How to hear this invitation to a wholesale rethinking of the collective inhabitation of North America? How to initiate a heretical friendship among peoples? The disaffiliated political affect in the writing of a few self-reflexive paupers provides some furtive indications of a tipping point on the other side of which the descendants of the old *Canadiens* may, finally, arrive in America, and accept the revolutionary impetus of the Circle. Sioui notably cites Savard in his 1989 work: "We no longer have a choice; it is that America [of the Great Circle] into which we must seriously consider disembarking, at last."[32]

What else would we wish to do, we who have political violence as our inheritance, we who still have empty hands?

6

The Eye of the Master
(Animal *Excursus*)

The source of our survival is also (at the end of the day)
the source of our paralysis.
Will we continue to pursue the foolishness
of this illegitimate accumulation, regardless?
According to what blind principle?
Robert Hébert[1]

Today more than ever the urgent question is: What does it mean to be a master? By extension, what does it mean to want to be a master, and what has this meant for "classic" Québécois political aspirations? What is the imaginary to which this desire to be masters in our own house is linked? What hidden code is lodged in the image of our own house? Here I follow some accidental contingencies surfacing from what might be called francophone cultural detritus – that compost flowing through our ordinary language, forming a constellation of meanings around the idea of the master.

From Poitou to the Côte-du-Sud

One winter evening as I was browsing through a friend's library, I discovered *À l'heure du loup*, an unclassifiable work by Pierre Morency.[2] The book immediately fascinated me. Morency was born in Lauzon (today, part of Lévis), in the working-class quarter of the maritime zone from which my family also hails, stretched across both sides of the Saint Lawrence. Morency lived on l'Île d'Orléans, on the river, in front of Saint-Michel, right where I found myself on that evening – the stars were aligned, as they say.

I came across a passage in which Morency narrates a travel story, through the voice of his persona, Trom. The story takes place in France:

> I asked the hotel employee what happened to Mr. B., that ruddy, loud Poitevin-ian I had met the day before at breakfast.[3] He was a jolly storyteller with a lively interest in everything concerning Quebec, since he had housed soldiers of the 22nd Regiment in 1944.[4]
>
> —Mr. B.? Oh, he left the same day. He is a farmer, you know. For years, once a month, always on the same date, he has come to town to visit his son at the Great Clinic. When he left, he said was off to do the master's-eye rounds.
>
> —The master's-eye rounds?
>
> —I was struck by the expression as well. He explained that a good farmer must do the rounds of his estate every day, to check on the state of the crops and the buildings, to check the animals' health by inspecting their fur, and such.
>
> Three hours later, in the library, rifling through a collection by Italo Calvino, *Last Comes the Raven*, on page 76, I fell upon a story entitled "The Master's Eye," which begins with the words, "The master's eye, his father told him, pointing to his own eye, the master's eye fattens the horse."[5]

Trom, Morency's persona, with whom I suddenly confused myself, learns about the ancient and very precise meaning of the figure of the master and the mastery through which he is defined. In fact, the eye of the master is an old story of the soil, grounded in the peasant imaginary and its motifs, running through the literature from Poitou, la Provence, and the Côte-du-Sud, that is to say, between France and Quebec, between Giono[6] and Morency.

What is this eye of the master about? What meaning does it carry? When the eye performs its surveilling action in the specific, very charged context of the farm, it is the eye belonging to the master of exploitation, the plantation, the enterprise, the eye that reassures itself, one might say, as to the health or – what is essentially the same thing – the productivity of these things. An essentially productive relation is revealed here – the process of "fattening"

Figure 6.1
On highway 640, north of Montreal.

entailing an ambiguous relationship, an extractivism that is systematically implanted at the heart of life itself, through breeding. The eye's radius of activity covers landed property, the scope of territory in the master's control. With this eye, the master secures his estate and profits from its maximized productivity.

The idea of a master's eye that surveils the land, the animals, the exploitation, the estate and its surrounding nature, an eye that renders farm animals profitable, "fattening" the horse, as if by magic, intersects in some way with a notion of care (thus we say "caring for the animals," "tending to the animals"). The idea of care does carry tender connotations, but it is not always or necessarily tender: there is an ordinary, normalized violence in it. Often there is cruelty in the exercise of mastery on a farm, as anyone familiar with the domestic lives of farmers knows. The frustrations attending this way of life are inscribed in the being of its immediate witnesses – children, hiding out in the corners of sheds; women, behind the curtains.[7] Jos-Phydime Michaud describes the *habitant*'s "aversion to animals" in *Kamouraska de mémoire*:

The few farmers who loved and petted their horses were mocked by the others. The mentality was not one conducive to loving animals. The horses were always worrisome, and yet much more would have been gained if we had been gentle. I saw impossible situations: guys charged with transporting loads of sand that were far too heavy for the horse and then severely beating the horses. No one was openly horrified by this, even though we did speak of it a few times. The children were not encouraged to love the animals, like today, in the cities, where the children pet cats and dogs. On the contrary, we threw stones at them. I was like the others: as soon as I saw wild game coming out of the forest, I grabbed a gun and fired. We had a kind of aversion toward animals.[8]

The eye of the master also evokes a very clear concept of *management*, an idea of control. As Marc Fumaroli observes of the rubric used for parts of the body, in his study of the "memory-bank of the French language" stored in expressions and metaphors:

Having an eye on, keeping an eye on, keeping a close eye on:[9] the eye, being active, drawing objects towards itself and having a radius of action, becomes the soul's policeman or spy in these expressions, an organ for focusing attention on worrisome objects and beings that could escape its control.[10]

The eye is an organ for controlling from a distance, a policeman, a spy. This eye evokes those Canadian soldiers of the 22nd Regiment in Morency's travel narrative, boarding in Poitou farms. This eye also brings to mind the image of a control tower, mechanically sweeping across a space with its luminous ray, or the visual capture of territory like the one expressed in the military conceptualization of space, as described by Paul Virilio in *Speed and Politics*:

Recent accounts have shown the relation between the limits of the clearing and that of human vision from an elevated site. The pioneer is more clearly called a *pathfinder* by the Anglo-Saxons. Land-clearing, the cultivation of the earth for subsistence, the receding of forest darkness, are in reality the creation of a military glacis as field of vision, of one of those frontier deserts spoken of by Julius Caesar, which, he says, represent the glory of the Empire because they are like a permanent invasion of the land by the dromocrat's look and, beyond this, because the speed of this vision – ideally without obstacles – causes *distances to approach*.[11]

The space of control is that which can be captured by a single glance of the imperial eye. It is the surface that can be covered by the speed requisite to military domination – and this speed is a relation between land-clearing and strike force.

The master, who makes himself so through the exercise of this vision, wishes to operate all those "worrisome objects and beings that could escape [his] control," while keeping them under his yoke. His eye is a ray capturing territory with proprietary and military intent, that is to say, with statist intent. The connection between land-clearing and invading army is the very propaedeutics of agriculture, of the installation of settlers to occupy territory in order to feed the armies, the bankers, and functionaries of the metropolis, thereby realizing the core of imperialism, the *nomos* of the earth.[12]

Mastery, an Object of Fabulation

The eye of the master, as I have suggested via Morency's anecdote, is a common metaphor in French literature. In the Jean de La Fontaine[13] fable of this title (*The Fables of La Fontaine*, book 4, fable 21), a stag takes refuge in a stable of oxen, seeking to hide from hunters. The oxen advise him to find another hiding place, saying their stable is not as safe as it seems. Nevertheless, they agree to keep the forest creature's presence among them a secret. Soon, the stag, having evaded the notice of both the servants and the overseer who have come to feed them, decides the moment is right to come out of hiding. An ox warns him:

> T'is well...;
> But stop, – our master, with his hundred eyes,
> Has yet to hold his keen review;
> 'Tis that, poor stag, I fear for you!

The master, "with his hundred eyes," arrives to do his rounds and, the fable's function being the illustration of tragic necessity, the unavoidable thing happens:

Too soon was recognised the trembling deer,
Each fell upon him with his long boar-spear
His pleading tears availed him not the least;
They take him, salt him, dress the wretched beast,
And many a neighbour shares with joy the feast.[14]

The master is the *seigneur*, man in the image of God. He is the proprietor, the one invested with God's power and mission; the one who profits from the exploitation of the land, the title-holder, and thereby the only one who really sees what is in his interest. In comparison, the servants and the overseer seem blind. The old master is the one who knows, the one for whom nothing escapes.

La Fontaine's inspiration for the fable of "The Eye of the Master" was a Latin narrative by the fabulist Phaedrus (born a slave in the Roman Empire), "The Stag and the Oxen" (book 2, fable 8). The latter's version, very close to that of La Fontaine, ends with the words: "This fable proves that, when it comes to his affairs, no one sees more clearly than the master." Here, in essence, is the argument of the tragedy of the commons, according to which anything held in common is untended and unproductive, and inevitably goes down the drain.

Accompanying the *seigneur*-proprietor's infallible seeing is a power to segregate creatures. Through this power, which is his alone and in his exclusive interest, he separates that "ranger of the forests free," the stag, from the domesticated beasts, the oxen. The oxen, for their part, do not try to enforce such a separation when the stag asks for shelter among them; neither does the stag when he addresses them in a common language; neither do the servants or the overseer, who do not distinguish between the cervine and the bovine when they visit the stable. The line between civilization and savagery belongs to the domestic master, the head of the estate; it stems from the power of the *seigneur*.

The identification of the stranger is relentless; the stag is tracked down and devoured. The master's hand is as important as his eye: he has the monopoly over legitimate violence and over the command to sacrifice. He is entitled with the privileges of both murder and prodigality: he kills, he produces, he feeds, and "many a neighbour shares with joy the feast." Like a state, the master monopolizes violence, guards the frontier, guarantees the well-being of "his" populations. He is the figure of "any one has had to die so that there is room for any one to be" *par excellence.*[15]

As for La Fontaine's "master, with his hundred eyes," in the fable that he borrows from Phaedrus the Thracian (who has borrowed it, in turn, from Aesop the Greek, that fabulist of the Occident), this figure is a reference to the Greek god Argus, also Panoptes, who gives us the expression "followed by the eyes of Argus." This mythological figure, added to Homer posthumously (Homer being but a name for a long oral tradition, in any case) and known in popular Greek parlance, belongs to the Greco-Roman French heritage – and thereby, through, its accidental extension, to a Québécois one. Argus eats human flesh; he is cannibalistic. His eyes still look out from the wings of the peacock, king of the birds. Here we find something like the root of the myth of the master's (necessary) violence. It descends from an association with a god, one who sees all, and an eater of humans, one who exercises the prerogative to sacrifice.

As is well-known, this image of the panoptic, all-seeing eye inspired Jeremy Bentham, the father of English utilitarianism, to develop the architectural scheme of the prison with a central tower from which inmates would feel themselves to be constantly surveilled. Bentham died in London in 1832. It was on the basis of Bentham's plan that Michel Foucault theorized the paradigm of contemporary surveillance society. Foucault was born in Poitou and died in Paris in 1984. These are the ramifications of the eye of the master, woven between the two metropoles of Canada.

One might associate the eye of the master and the man with the hundred eyes with the Christian symbol of the all-seeing eye, as well – the eye that is sometimes seen above church altars. As the fanciful and erudite René Guénon[16] wrote on this score, in a text originally published in 1948:

> The upright triangle relates to the Principle; but when it is inverted by reflection in manifestation, the gaze of the eye which it contains appears to be directed somewhat downwards, that is, from the Principle towards manifestation itself; and besides its general meaning of "omnipresence," it then takes on more clearly the special sense of "Providence."[17]

Argus of the hundred eyes is replaced here by the unique and omniscient God, the god of confession whom the Catholics of the Saint Lawrence River valley knew so well, to the point of nausea. The omnipresent Lord, incorporating the Greco-English image of the panoptic, also models the terrestrial feudal landowner in his own image. The idea of Providence, here, takes on the teleological place of the tragic principle represented by the cannibalistic Argus. Providence substantivizes a kind of necessity in the order of the world, the necessity of the sacrificial power of masters.

One final element in this allegory of the eye of the master is revealed in the last sentence of La Fontaine's fable, taken from Phaedrus:

The master's eye the best surveys.
But I prefer the lover's piercing gaze.[18]

It is important to understand that, as Fumaroli observes, the "lover is also the master, the stag, the rival, the livestock, the jealously possessed mistress."[19] While exegesis may find something pleasing in this recurrence, if we are attuned to the intricacies of power relations, what is apparent is that the relation between the master and the beast is a (clearly erotic) relation of absolute possession corresponding to the legal relationship between the master of the estate (the *seigneur*) and his living possessions: wife, children, servants, serfs, animals, land, and water sources. Here we have the whole roman structure of the *domus*, antiquity's agricultural model, at the top of which rests the power to feed large numbers. The master of the estate, the free man, is owner and lord of a little fenced, productive world and its output. He has lined this world through the human domestication of nature. This is written in law; it is also part of the philosophical tradition, from Aristotle to John Locke.

The master of the estate, engaged in erotic pursuit of living possessions, a kind of reproducer-in-chief, distrusts his own domesticated world. It is inferior: its creatures do not possess reason, at least not the reason of a master (or what is today called "business sense," in the language of politicians). The master with an eye for business, with vision, must control this domestic universe in order to ensure its smooth functioning, seeing as he is in charge of everyone's well-being, but he exerts this control for his own benefit as well – and for the benefit of the society of patriarchs and their estates. They are all linked together in the food chain of collective title-holders, the organ for the capture of surplus, which they prefer to call the state.[20]

"L'Abitation de Quebecq"

The state, deconstructed and reduced to its most elementary form, is a stronghold, a walled garden, a stockyard, operated by a host of servants and overseen by a master who gives it its political and legal personality. In the context of Quebec's imperial foundations, the idea of the master's estate may call to mind "l'abitation de Quebecq" built at Stadacona in 1608 in what is taken to be the "founding moment" of the first European government on the great river of Canada. In Samuel de Champlain's account of 1608, he writes:

> On the first of October I had some wheat sown and on the fifteenth some rye. On the third of the month there was a white frost and on the fifteenth the leaves of the trees began to fall. On the twenty-fourth of the month I had some native vines planted and they prospered extremely well, but after I left the settlement to come back to France, they were all ruined for want of care, which very much distressed me.[21]

According to the received imaginary, Champlain's habitation *represents* the first estate of New France, with Champlain as the first master, providing a model for the colonial relation to territory. During the first winter, the French residing at the settlement are ravaged by scurvy. The ruins of the habitation lie beneath the existing Place Royale in Quebec City, close to the site which Champlain and his men believed to be the habitation built by Jacques Cartier, before them: a chimney, foundations, a surrounding pit, squared timber, canon balls – "all these things show clearly that this was a settlement which was founded by Christians," Champlain writes.[22]

It is not as if the foot of the cape (where Quebec City now stands) was not already inhabited; it was, and Champlain's narrative mentions this fact: "Meanwhile many of the natives had encamped near us, who used to fish for eels."[23] Oral tradition is very explicit about seasonal Innu presence in the region of Quebec City (Uepishtikueiau), the Baie de Beauport, l'Île d'Orléans, and the mouth of the Cabircoubat (Saint Charles) river.[24] Innu prized these sites as places for hunting migratory birds, in addition to fishing eel. At the mouth of the river, their oral tradition recalls, one found a forest of walnut trees, sturgeon, salmon, porpoise, sea wolves, bustards, geese, ducks, teal, cranes, wild raspberries, herds of eastern wapiti, and turtles (the latter two species now extinct due to overhunting), and birchbark thick enough for canoe making. In short, it was a meeting place, a place for celebrations, matrimonial and political alliances, the launching of warrior expeditions against the Haudenosaunee, via the Richelieu River or the upper Saint Lawrence. Oral tradition demonstrates that the Iroquoian sites described by Cartier in his exploration narratives were known by the Innu of the seventeenth century. The Innu left the Quebec City area at the end of every October in order hunt along the river's tributaries. As early as 1630, it is said, the region was becoming inhospitable, as the fauna were departing.

From the point of view of Champlain, or what we might call the eye of the master, it was necessary to exclude Innu who appeared at the door of the habitation. The fortress inaugurated a new, gated interiority, grounded in the distinction between civilization and savagery, and reinforced by the founder's grotesque anecdotes and their insistence on the indigence of the Innu who wintered nearby. In Champlain's narrative, the habitation becomes a theatre for the mise-en-scène of the supposed rudeness of Innu nomadic customs: they eat the rotten meat that the French toss from their fortification, he observes. The so-called "*sauvages*," seen from a small portal in the habitation, are for Champlain reduced to scavengers. His fantasy-laden depiction draws on the Hobbesian figure of the savage, characterized by his lack of a state and resulting terror of enemy attack:

> The whole time they were with us, which was for them the safest place, they were in such constant dread of their enemies, that they often took fright at night in their dreams, and would send their wives and children to our fort, the gates of which I used to have opened for them, but let the men remain about the fort, not permitting them to enter, for they were as safe there as to their persons as if they had been inside. And I used to send out five or six of our men to give them courage, and to go and search the woods whether they could see anything, which used to

satisfy them. They are very timid and fear their enemies greatly, and hardly ever sleep quietly wherever they are, although I reassured them every day as much as I could, by admonishing them to do as we did.[25]

The inhabitants of the region were "with us," Champlain says, indicating that for him this was already, without regard for the 1603 alliance with the Wendat and Anishinaabeg nations at Tadoussac point, the territory of the French. The Innu were dependent on others, reliant on French protection. Innu men, in particular, were to be kept outside in the manner of the stag in La Fontaine's fable. Oral tradition indicates that the Innu themselves were quick to grasp this: "They built a garden, surrounded by a fence which they continuously extended, until the Innu left to hunt."[26]

Champlain's habitation is a kind of cross between the ancient agricultural estate and the military fort. The domanial architecture of the agricultural estate and the military fort erected for the defense of a walled territory: forms suited to master's eye, together providing the model for old French Canada's territorial occupation, from the west of the island of Montreal to the south shore and Domaine-du-Roy. The fort, which finds a correspondent in the trading posts dotting the landscape from the Saint Lawrence to Hudson's Bay and on to the Red River, inscribes itself indelibly in the North American colonial topological imaginary.

This topography instigates the fantasy of being surrounded on all sides, which we find as much in the British-American imaginary[27] as in the franco one and which, via the cultural construct of the Iroquois attack, gives us the Québécois "in our own house."[28] In this fantasy, the settlers barricade themselves in, defending civilization while the natives are all around, coming from everywhere in order to destroy it. Stefano Harney and Fred Moten provide critical reflection on this topography and the fantasy it contains in a passage commenting on the Western in *The Undercommons*. "In Michael Parenti's classic anti-imperial analysis of Hollywood movies, he points to the 'upside down' way that the 'make-believe media' portrays colonial settlement. In films like *Drums Along the Mohawk* (1939) or *Shaka Zulu* (1987), the settler is portrayed as surrounded by "natives," inverting, in Parenti's view, the role of aggressor so that colonialism is made to look like self-defense."[29] In this fantasy, the settlers become the victims of the savage hordes prowling around the village gates.

As the Innu explain, Champlain's occupation of Quebec and the violence Innu suffered at the hands of the French eventually led them to avoid the region entirely and retreat to the Côte-Nord. The surviving women of the Quebec region integrated themselves into other Innu groups. Oral tradition thus attests to settler violence towards Indigenous peoples, violence that is inverted by the fantasy of the surrounded fort. But oral tradition also provides evidence of a resilience that Harney and Moten mobilize as they offer a new inversion of the fantasmatic relation between white and racialized people, between civilization and savagery:

> Indeed, aggression and self-defense are reversed in these movies, but the image of a surrounded fort is not false. Instead, the false image is what emerges when a critique of militarised life is predicated on the forgetting of the life that surrounds it. The fort really was surrounded, is besieged by what still surrounds it, the common beyond and beneath – before and before – enclosure. The surround antagonizes the laager in its midst while disturbing that facts on the ground with some outlaw planning.[30]

There is no better example of outlaw planning, beyond the reach of the master's eye, than Indigenous resistance past and present, poised against the colonial state with its destructive domestications and laws of enclosure.

Apikunakanu

This *excursus* has traced the slogan's chronic reappearance as a kind of colonial spectre on the banks of the Saint Lawrence. The image of the eye of the master is inscribed in the law and ontology of the seigneurial imaginary through which empire was transferred from France to North America in the seventeenth century. The image travels from Greek and Roman antiquity to the Christian mental landscape, carrying the oldest associations of political and territorial power, what we might call the arcana of occidental power. The figure of the master is, in this sense, one of the keys to the structure of political thought found at the imperial foundation, that is to say, vernacular Québécois culture. Unsurprisingly, the figure has found a place at the heart of the imaginary of political reconquest for Canadians of Old, in the formula "masters in our own house."

In the last third of the eighteenth century, the French master departed and, in accordance with the principle of the eternal return of the master that we might also term "Providence," the omniscient eye, now the British military and commercial elite, surveilled the territory from the heights of Quebec City and along the estates on the banks of the Saint Lawrence, to the townships set up to capture forest and mining resources south of the river and to the northwest, on the Pays-d'en-Haut side. The first action of the British master was to create an enclave that, in the context of a more dispersed francophone presence in America, would enframe the old French Canadians within the limits of the "Government of Quebec" as laid out by the Royal Proclamation of 1763. At the same time, the Royal Proclamation would establish the regime of land cessation for his majesty's "Indian" nations, a regime that prefigured the reserve system and the numbered treaties[31] and put in place the contemporary system of legal dispossession that modern Quebec has inherited under the aegis of the Dominion of Canada. We now find ourselves on board the francophone flagship of the "Province of Quebec," that post-British, super-sized "*abitation de Quebecq.*"

Naomi Fontaine recalls that at the moment that the Uashat reserve was created near Sept-Îles, in Nitassinan (which the Québécois call Côte-Nord), the Innu were literally enclosed:

> With the establishment of the reserve, the government thought best to erect a high metal fence to demarcate the border that the Innu would not be able to cross without a valid reason, from now on. They were so close to the newcomers. There was only a verge of trees and some waste ground between them. They weren't dangerous. They were disorderly. Unpredictable. Free. From the temperate boreal forest to the icy tundra. Their paths were not inscribed on any map. Neither were their departures inscribed on any calendar. It was the seasons that influenced their movement.[32]

The British Empire's practice of enclosing populations was perhaps all too easily absorbed into the Québécois seigneurial imaginary inherited from

France. In that imaginary, as we have seen, the master's eye keeps within its purview everything it would control.[33] It is the eye of the proprietor. The fence and the enclosure belong to its sphere of action and control: mastery of production, the productivity of the land and the productivity of living beings. A legacy of the French colonial era, this theory of the enterprise seems natural to the populations "required for the purpose of settlement," installed in the provincial enclosure. While the Québécois do not inherit a French colonial prerogative – however much they may wish to maintain that they do – they nevertheless do inherit the imaginary carrying the arcana of this medieval and, at root, Greco-Roman form of power, hierarchical by design and authoritarian by default.

Within this enclosure erected by the federal government in the process of carrying out its global project of "civilizing savages," the Innu – who become "worrisome," "disorderly," and "unpredictable" beings in the eyes of the Québécois – can be kept under watch. As Fontaine writes: "Having built the reserve, they were necessarily afraid. I speak of the builders, of course."[34] "The builders": a name, on the Côte-Nord, given to the descendants of working-class Québécois who have populated the towns north of the Saint Lawrence since the 1950s. In the rhetoric of the current government of Quebec, the same builders are referred to as our "elders," those who "built Quebec." They are, in a sense, the workers on the estate, the hired men and their families, the mercenaries sent north by the colonial capital to erect enterprises where, in the eye of the master, there is nothing at all. As in Champlain's version, nothing but scavengers and thick forests: this is the sum, for him, of the "temperate boreal forest," the seasons and movements, described in Fontaine's version.

The builders are my countrymen, my cousins, my neighbours; they are the "frogs," the "pea soups," the minor whites, the rigadoon-dancing hired men, bored and lonely at the Manic dam worksite, the mortgaged laics who feed at Costco. They are the residue of the original colonizing population, whom the british-canadian master long has cast as a pseudo-people, an avatar, material for assimilation, shaping a self-image perhaps only reinforced by the sovereigntist expressions "lost referenda" and "stolen nation." There is a doubt which insists, encysts, "*incysts*."[35] Are the builders really masters? Are they not, at root, only oxen, poor beasts worn down by the yoke, blistered by the saddle, seeking to be something other than oxen in a stable, wishing to get out, even if only to be valets, or to glory in the fact that at least one of them has managed to take the place of the master?

If the builders willingly identify with the cry "masters in our own house" then perhaps it is because they have some doubts as to their own mastery. Perhaps they are secretly comforted by the fence the master has installed in order to enclose the nomads in their own territory, thereby reactivating a foundational fear expressed in the anxious demarcation of savagery and civilization, and the walling off of the unpredictable and disorderly. Shutting the stags into the enclosure, importing oxen to perform the arduous labour (but never too many, lest they destroy our culture), and taking the place of the master in his house: this is the program for mastery, tailor-made to the northeast of North America. Tracking down the stag in the stable is a bit like tracking down the woman in a veil: it amounts to adopting the master's eye, becoming the "man with the hundred eyes," exercizing the privilege of sacrificing the Indigenous and the refugee. Masters in our own house: a predatory form of attention.

Turning, once again, to Naomi Fontaine:

I was asked what I thought the most beautiful word in the French language was. Here it is:

Liberté.

It is a word that does not actually exist in my language. Liberty is a concept intrinsic to everything that exists in our vision of the world. We come from a space without fences, without borders. Beings who are free from childhood on, from the very moment we become autonomous. Even animals are not captured in order to be bred. It is a condition that has never had to be named.

The only way of saying liberty in Innu-aimun is to name the end of an incarceration.

Apikunakanu.[36]

There are no terms for liberty in Innu other than the word that corresponds to emancipation or liberation, because liberty itself is a fact, a "concept intrinsic to everything that exists in our vision of the world." *Apikunakanu* corresponds, more precisely, to freeing oneself, since one may be held or hindered. One may be detained, even captured. Always, though, there is liberty, like the very air breathed, since it is the fundamental condition of things, it is what they are: free. As Pierrot Ross-Tremblay puts it:

> When I say I am Innu, I invoke the most ancient and meaningful sense of "being human." The word reveals an unfathomable richness of values founded in a radical respect for the human, for freedom, for every form of life; it is a philosophy of the human that implies a way of life in tune with that which maintains it, in other words, a capacity to nourish what nourishes.[37]

The Québécois who dreams of independence via the inherited means of colonial disinheritance envies the master's ease and big house. He wants to get out of the stable, but only in order to enter the big house and climb the ladder of mastery, supported in this vain effort by his domestic personnel, dependents, possessions, animals, fields, house, car, equipment, chalet, skidoo, vacation packages, gear, beauties, stumpage fees, hunting permits, studies, trips, start-ups, senior citizens, immigrants, Indigenous peoples. If he were to leave the stable, he would only buy a stable for himself. What else would he do? The Québécois ox has not yet arrived in America; he hasn't even put his nose outside, like the dairy cow that lives and dies in the stable without even sniffing the air, while providing the milk for international prize-winning cheeses.

And when the master seizes the stag in the stable, the oxen – silent, resigned, perhaps even relieved – facilitate his killing. Providence is saved; the man with the hundred eyes really does see all. What is more, all is well in the stable. When there's a master, we're taken care of. It's terrifying to live outside of the stable. We're not wild animals! We're not about to run for our food! As for all the parks and fences, they're inevitable, it's progress. After all, whom do these stag take themselves for, not wanting a stable? Why would they want something we don't have, we who have sacrificed so much for the master and for

Providence? The world itself is a stable and we are in it, we want to be in it. So, if necessary, we'll kill the stag ourselves! Long live the master! Long live the stable! Long live our "we"!

• • •

According to popular belief, a twitching eye means that someone is thinking of us. The eye of the little Laurentian master, it seems to me, is quivering, maybe even folding in on itself. Meanwhile, there are dissonant sounds coming from the nooks and crannies of memory consciousness, like the taste of beauty. Perhaps, without meaning to, we are recalling how pleasant it is to take to the woods.

To play about, unwravel, dig around in the gear of the bastard-colonial imaginary in order to find routes to disidentification from the state: living, itinerant paths through the ruins of the supersized PQ *domus*. To find an opening for talk between the oxen and the stags, between the cattle and the deer; to find refuge; to block the hundred eyes of the master with pine gum, to burn the stable.

A Conclusion in Erratic Blocs

We still have not brought to light, from beneath the tired robes of our cultural fatigue, the fabulous part of our intimate dispossession. But can we see this Daimon within us, this poetic and vital, anonymous, idiotic, and inspired part, this unrecognized character of ours, without prescribing its image, and, especially, without turning it into a little interior god through which our identitarian narcissism might be redeemed?

Frédérique Bernier[1]

Accident

What should we make of the fact that, no matter who we are, we are here, we have come through here, we are of here, we are of here as elsewhere, we are from elsewhere? What should we make of this place in its absolute singularity and its radical contingency, its complexity, its palimpsest of cultures, and how, therefore, shall we inhabit it? How shall we invent a fitting hospitality?

As I have suggested in the preceding essays, it is time to face the necessity of acknowledging and assuming our position, in all of its historical and geographical entanglements, including what is paradoxical and a source of suffering in it. We must acknowledge the structure and hierarchy that persists in our collective and linked trajectories, in order to move toward a more ethical version of culture.

This requires, of everyone, here, now, that we share our histories: histories of violence, of failure, of improbable movement; also histories of survival, of small victories over the self and over the official victors. This way, we can

contribute to a history from below, not a popular history for the edification
of the nation, but a history of histories, a choral history of becoming-minor
in America.[2] This history from below must, at the same time, tell of failed aspirations, of the consequences of striving to incarnate exclusive power and
dictate the order of things, as we took ourselves for kings, constructing an
identity and gold plating our teeth.

Georges E. Sioui suggests that we speak of the colonization of the Americas
in terms of accident rather than discovery, "contact," or encounter. Contemporary settler-colonial Quebec – to put it bluntly – originates in a series of
accidents.[3] Jacques Cartier was searching for the Indies for the benefit of a
French monarch. The fur trade generated further interest among emissaries
and shareholders, as did the exploitation of sugar cane in the Antilles. Getting
one's hands on this gold mine and then defending it required European settlement designed to perpetuate the infrastructure of imperial capture. There
was recourse to indentured labour and military garrisons in order to maintain
an essentially extractive colony. Afterwards, in order to people the valley of
the Saint Lawrence, there were policies for retaining indentured labourers and
the soldiers having neither attachments nor capital. The *habitants*, artisans,
and day labourers left behind by France in the moment of the conquest (and
never asked for their opinion) were then fairly easily mobilized in the service
of the colonial enterprise conducted by the British Empire, explicitly aimed
at settling North America.

The population descended from this European enterprise sought to defend
the country it had fashioned within this frame, for good and ill, and as the aux-
illary of the major powers. It sought to defend francophone and Catholic life
"as we know it" (or, as it is now known, in the post-9/11 era, life according to
"Western values"). But especially, it sought to defend life "as we know it": in
other words, life with no project beyond seeing to one's own business, fattening
one's livestock, satisfying one's socio-economic pride – no project beyond en-
joying one's foothold and protecting it from those who would contest it.

It is a world of men, a world of workers, a world of small proprietors that
was built up and fixed in this way. It is a world without foundations other
than what is "good for business," other than the well-stocked larder, the girls
married off, the absence of a better offer. The Québécois descended from the
French regime demonstrate a visceral rooting in place, the feeling of those
who have nowhere else to go and have not chosen to be here. This is what is
prolonged and spun out into a sublimated, collective, almost poetic form with

the Quiet (Industrial) Revolution. It is this enduring feeling that accounts for our election, for two decades, of Quebec governments that Julia Posca describes, with irony, as "parvenu": "The parvenu knows neither rest nor felicity, is always ahead, dragging society along in a vertiginous, limitless ascent. His quest produces affluence, prosperity, and fecundity, and takes us absolutely nowhere, at lightning speed."[4]

It is about a world that is both accidental and real, the only known world, a world that cannot be imagined otherwise, even though there is much missing and even though the reasons for being here stem from administrative decisions, ordinary miseries, the movements of capital. Being here, for no reason, egoistically, serving the powers that be, in succession, getting to the end of the month, taken by surprise and yet proud when the kids become educated, speak English, travel by plane, feel at home in the twenty-first century. "In Québec, this is how we live," affirmed the premier, François Legault, tautologically, as justification for a policy that bans the veil while passing itself off as a law on securalism.

In order to survive the global accident that is colonialism, it seems there is a need to create a sense of necessity, crystallize our privilege, invent reasons as we go, even at the risk of borrowing them from others and from the more powerful. Even at the risk of lying to ourselves a bit about what we are, and indefinitely postponing recognition of this place in which we find ourselves. Mathieu Bélisle, articulating the dominance of "ordinary life" in the Québécois ethos, puts it this way: "I cannot relinquish this supplementary meaning and value for which I can find neither a source nor an exact image; it lives in me like the echo of a lost world, or one that was never really known."[5]

There's a story to be told here, a story of the affects of power, a story of domination in settler-colonial America that is at once banal and incredible and, as it is in the nature of these things to do, goes nowhere. It begins with wandering and accident.

Contiguity

Within the singular space-time of Quebec, how to break open the mortifying political matrix that ossifies our lives into a project somewhere between the petro-electric liquidation of collective space-time (global ecocide) and the compulsively paranoid self-barricading of closed borders (nationalist racism)?

By what route, and in the name of what forces, shall we refuse this geopolitical and existential project, which has become so total?

As Malcom Ferdinand points out, decolonization cannot set aside ecological issues without risking collapse into the very pursuit of imperial destruction that defines modernity:

> Decolonization in the Americas suffered from the same modern double fracture. Because colonization and the colonial situation was understood to refer exclusively to the control of a foreign administration over an indigenous (or local) people, the various anticolonial movements of the eighteenth to the twentieth century essentially worked towards the recovery of a sovereignty proper to these peoples. By dissociating the fate of landscapes and ecosystems from how colonialism is understood, anticolonialism developed without altering the relationship of intensive exploitation of the land. This has often translated into the desire of becoming the master in place of the master, of being the one who profits from colonial inhabitation.[6]

In short, there is no decolonization without a radical reconsideration of the relationship to the earth that is at the centre of the European colonial enterprise.

This is exactly what the Indigenous theorists and activists of North America have been saying to us for a long time and what the Atikamekw and Montagnais Council articulated very clearly in 1978, for the buccaneer ministers of the first Lévesque government gathered at the Château Frontenac, when they described what the arrival of Europeans in the Saint Lawrence valley meant for them:

> The regions in which we could continue to live in our way and where white civilization was only a few small fishing villages, settlers or *coureurs de bois*, allowed a certain harmony with the white man, since he lived close to nature, like us, and his way of life was not so far from our own.

> But you decided to further exploit and to establish your technology, your principles, your habits, your rules, and your laws wherever you could, taking more and more of what belonged to us, without concern for our

habits, our customs, and our way of life, all of which had been ours for millenia before your arrival.

In the name of your "civilization" and your appetite for profit, you have exploited our forests, lakes, and rivers, without heed of any consequences. You have erected dams, implanted mining and forestry companies, constructed railways and electrical lines in the very places from which we gain our sustenance.[7]

Thus, when "the white man ... lived close to nature" in "a few small fishing villages," trading and engaging in subsistence agriculture, some harmony was possible. According to the Atikamekw and Innu representatives, it was industrialization of the Saint Lawrence valley and the creation of resource regions over the course of the twentieth century that upset the equilibrium between the different forms of life possible, up to that point, as well as destroying the diversity of forms of life in the territory.

This destruction was in the name of the capitalist state-form that colonialism invariably delivers (contemporary history, in a nutshell), the state-form into which the French Canadians–become–"Québécois masters of their own house" have led themselves through accidental wandering and ferocious identification. The capitalist state-form is the nerve that contemporary decolonial struggle strikes, as we have seen with the recent Wet'suwet'en resistance in British Columbia.

Because colonial civilization destroys the sources and places of life itself, theorizing colonialism requires an equivalent attention to the racism grounding all the forms of dehumanization produced as a matter of necessity within this colonial frame: what you have to do to live, what you have to destroy in order to create, the sacrifice you have to justify, the few eggs you have to break to make the omelette – so much cynical evidence of the cruelties committed in the name of a particular organization of collective life. The question of our use of the land, of the ontological and epistemological frame that fuels our ways of living and inhabiting, home-making and place-making, communicating and educating is intrinsically tied to issues of racism, sexism, and exploitation. Our relationship to the land establishes an entire order of necessity, all the hierarchies derived from this order, and the dominations that crystallize within it. What is needed is a general strike against multiform colonialism.

One act was performed in Montreal in 1969, when students tossed computer lab equipment into the street at Sir George Williams University (now Concordia) in order to protest racism at the institution.

What is this capitalist-colonial order of necessity, which requires the construction of dams on distant rivers – where human groups have fished for millenia, sustaining themselves and (re)creating their cultures – all for the sake of electrical power that is not even needed in the Saint Lawrence valley? This is the very order that needs to be put into question and so it is a question of global justice that is posed here, a difficult question, to be sure, but one which has become unavoidable. At stake in this question is the destruction of the earth, the destruction of peoples. There is a connection between the historical servitude of statist populations and colonial racism, and this connection must be insisted upon, again and again.

Here, today, if we are to slip through the mesh of the colonial-national-global net, we must relinquish all claims to its spoils; we must give up the prize money, cease to identify with the fruits of colonialism, the multiform structure of dispossession from which we draw our subsistence, albeit poorly and unequally. Because this taking only replaces the emptiness that haunts the Québécois pauper of settler colonialism, covering over the lack of foundation, the lack of a legitimate relation to territory. A panacea for accidentalism; the spoils of colonialism are rotten fruit indeed.

Thus a local decolonial strategy, striking at the heart of Quebec's colonial imaginary, would involve assembling the symbolic methods and materials required to desert Champlain's *domus*, abandon the master's house, cease calling ourselves "hydro-Québécois," and derail the machine for colonial capture of which we consist, here, today.

The indentured labourers, the soldiers, the accidents of colonialism, the "populations required for the purposes of settlement," can always, at any moment, demobilize themselves, refuse the mandates of empire, conspire, dream of freedom, take to the woods, return to their wandering, seek horizontal encounters with others, or maroon themselves, as Ferdinand puts it. They can accept their losses, accept bankruptcy, and inaugurate other ways of inhabiting – permitting themselves the fantasy of arriving in America about 500 years late. Being without foundation, or cause, their empty hands are the very symptom of this possibility, this chance waiting to be seized. In the register of political economy, this is what Yves-Marie Abraham proposes in a manner that is both tentative and implacable:

> If we really value life, justice, and freedom, we have no choice but to abolish the business enterprise, or at least allow it only the most marginal place in our lives. This means we also must do away with its essential elements: notably, the wage, private property, and the dissociation of the labour of production from the labour of reproduction. It should become possible for humans to live without being constrained to sell their labour power for a wage, and without the obligation to contribute to the accumulation of capital through the production of commodities. This supposes that it will eventually become impossible for the "means of production" to be the exclusive property of a small minority of human beings and to be accumulated without limit. As well, it supposes that those means be used, first and foremost, not in the production of commodities but in order to live, with the primary goal being the reproduction of our existence as well as that of the other living beings peopling this planet. And this labour of reproduction, as well as the resources necessary to it, must be shared equitably among humans, with respect for the life of non-human beings.[8]

How to live in such a way that life is not lived as an enterprise? How to live other than in blind service to the agents of colonialism, and without becoming one of those colonizing agents oneself? These are urgent questions, which the mercenary patriarchy of Québécois builders has never, does not, and will never address, not even while the ship is sinking. Meanwhile, others, from all around, are responding to precisely these questions.

So: Let's return to Sainte-Barbe, to the space below deck on the ships carrying the hired men of New France. Below deck, and yet above the hold where the Africans were chained on their way to slavery in the Caribbean. Let's find another possible course. Let's place ourselves, politically, under the impetus of the Circle, in the very deepest sense. This might be a way of renewing our hearts and minds, ensuring our own humility, forcing us, finally, to come to terms with reality. It is at this point zero of disembarkment that it might be possible to reconstruct the imaginary of the paupers of settler colonialism

and begin to build a chain of solidarity between living beings, in homage to
accident and contiguity, and on the basis of a radical, horizontal, polymorphous practice of sharing the earth:

> before the fall of night
> you would like to arrive
> somewhere
> the spirit renewed
> a fly on each of your knees[9]

Friendship

Réjean Ducharme,[10] in his sad and very beautiful novel in verse, *The Daughter
of Christopher Columbus*, provides a figure embodying the perspective of a
decolonial politics of disinheritance. In this passage, the animal friends of
Columbia Columbus, who are accompanying her around the world, ponder
her intentions:

> The goose and the pachyderm keep each other company.
> "I wonder where we're headed," says the more ferocious one
>   [a rhinoceros].
> "Columbia won't give us any trouble."
> Are they being led to a hecatomb or to a wedding?
>
> "I for one have complete confidence in her.
> I think that she's taking us nowhere.
> Columbia has been a vagabond since her childhood
> And she will wander until the hour of her death.
>
> To produce nothing is her mission."[11]

In Ducharme's nihilist fantasy, Columbia is the daughter of the "discoverer"
of the Americas, the sacred Columbus of 1492, who died without knowing
that he had landed in America rather than Asia. Columbus has died from
swallowing too much fish in his insular retirement. Having exploited his

daughter's labour and thought only of himself, never of others, he has stuffed himself to death. As for his daughter, Columbia, it is possible to "have complete confidence in her," her goose friend says, because "to produce nothing is her mission." Columbia is a wanderer. Her hands are empty and she does not question this condition; it is part of a whole other quest, a whole other set of customs and manners linked to beauty and relationship, a quest that is without judgement but also without compromise. Friendship's embrace has placed her with the animals rather than, and in spite of, the "humans." Her *motus*, the impulse she figures, is a stubborn, childlike, heretical refusal of all forms of violence. "Radical refusal through a paradoxical immobility, as in the flight of an arrow: time is suspended, and recovered."[12]

What Columbia Columbus represents – along with the animals, the project of producing nothing, the project of not having a project, of being poor without a plan – is not individual, or national, or narrowly political. What her condition figures, rather, is a tipping point, a zone of indeterminacy, the possibility of jamming colonial time – which is also a multitude of potential openings onto another agenda, for vital existence, and for bursting the eye of the master.

Notes

TRANSLATOR'S INTRODUCTION

1 Jean de La Fontaine, *The Fables of La Fontaine*, trans. R. Thomson (London: J. C. Nimmo and Bain, 1884), 98. The lines attributed to Phaedrus at the end of La Fontaine's version have been translated in different ways. Elizur Wright, for instance, translates them as "The master's is the eye to see:– / I add the lover's, as for me." *The Fables of La Fontaine*, trans. Elizur Wright, ed. J. W. M. Gibbs (London: G. Bell, 1882). https://www.gutenberg.org/files/7241/7241-h/7241-h.htm.

2 Ibid.

3 Marc Fumaroli makes this suggestion about the connection between the lover and the reader in an endnote commenting on the lines attributed to Phaedrus. Marc Fumaroli, *La Fontaine: Fables*, vol. 1, bks. 1–4 (Paris: Imprimerie nationale, 1985), 385.

4 "The Stag Among the Cattle," trans. [from Phaedrus] by Laura Gibbs, *Aesop's Fables* (Oxford: Oxford University Press, 2002), 161.

5 Lauren Berlant, *Cruel Optimism* (Duke University Press, 2011) 20. Berlant responds to what she sees as "the need to invent new genres for the kinds of speculative work we call 'theory'" by paying attention to anarchist anti-neoliberal art activisms "that aim to disrupt the contemporary political sensorium" and its "normative affect management styles," which include attachment to the "nation/state as optimistic object," 19–20. See also Andrew Brooks, "Glitch/Failure: Constructing a Queer Politics of Listening," *Leonardo Music Journal*, "The Politics of Sound Art," 25 (2015): 37–40.

6 Berlant, *Cruel Optimism*, 21. Giroux cites the influence of queer of colour critique and the work of the trans theorist Paul B. Preciado. Personal communication with the author, December 2021.

7 In a recollection of a conversation with the artist Moyra Davey, Giroux writes: "Moyra asks me to talk about this idea, the revolutionary question of jouissance. I respond: 'life is a process of learning – in situ.' Like … the character of the learned idiot, experimenters of the self are owls who long to look at the sun." Dalie Giroux, "Correspondences: Notes on the Art of Moyra Davey," trans. Andrea Kunard, *I Confess/J'Avoue* (Ottawa: National Gallery of Canada; Brooklyn: Dancing Foxes Press, 2020), 142.

8 Giroux, personal correspondence with the author, December 2021.

9 Giroux contributed an essay on Gilles Deleuze's version of Kafka to her first co-edited volume, the collection of essays entitled *Contr'hommage pour Gilles Deleuze*, edited with René Lemieux and Pierre-Luc Chenier (Quebec City: Presses de l'Université Laval, 2009).

10 The hens, Giroux writes, "have the habit of getting together under the house's front porch. They much prefer this spot to their large coop, and even to the cedar under which they also like to gather to take advantage of the shade and solace of the tree. They hang out lazily in the high summer sun like old women at the seaside." Giroux, "Correspondences," 148.

11 See Jean-François Nadeau's tribute to Levasseur in *Le Devoir*. https://www.ledevoir.com/opinion/chroniques/127269/en-aparte-lire-autre-chose.

12 This commitment to rethinking the boundaries of political studies is evident in the call to reflexivity that provides the rationale for the collection *Ceci n'est pas une idée politique: Réflexions sur les approches à l'étude des idées politiques*, eds. Dalie Giroux and Dimitrios Karmis (Quebec City: Presses de l'Université Laval, 2013). At UQAM, Giroux studied with Lawrence Olivier, Jean-Marc Piotte, and Thierry Hentsch.

13 The research creation and art activism collectives with which Giroux has been affiliated are Montreal based: the Concordia University–based SenseLab, the group Entrepreneurs du commun (organized to stage interventions in relation to Canada's Monument to the Victims of Communism), and the Atelier de géopoétique.

14 Mémoire d'encrier has been at the forefront of publishing minoritized, immigrant, second-generation and Indigenous authors in Quebec, building a catalogue of award-winning poetry, autobiography, fiction, historiography,

cultural and political critique, and translation, which includes Innu authors and authors from Africa, the Middle East, and the Caribbean. Mémoire d'encrier has published some of the most prominent Indigenous writers in Quebec, including a number of bilingual Innu/French works by the Innu poet Joséphine Bacon.

15 [Translation] Jenny Langevin, review of Dalie Giroux's *Le Québec brûle en enfer* (2017), in *L'Action nationale, Les cahiers de lecture*, December 2017. https://www.action-nationale.qc.ca/tous-les-articles/335-numeros-publies-en-2017/decembre-2017/comptes-rendus-de-decembre-2017/1153-dalie-giroux-le-quebec-brule-en-enfer.

16 [Translation] Marie-Paule Grimaldi, "Crever l'œil du maître: Ouvrir es chemins vers la décolonisation," 10 December 2020. http://www.magazine-spirale.com/article-dune-publication/crever-loeil-du-maitre-ouvrir-des-chemins-vers-la-decolonisation.

17 David Dorais, reviewing *L'œil du maître* for *L'Inconvenient*, describes Giroux's account of the summit at the Château Frontenanc in 1978, at which the arrogance of the Lévesque government caused First Nations leaders to leave in disgust after two days, "the defining moment in the history of botched opportunities for alliance." Dorais, "Rompre avec le colonialisme?," *L'Inconvénient* 85 (2021): 58. [Translation]

18 An Antane Kapesh's work has been translated into English recently by Sarah Henzi. See Kapesh, *Eukuan nin matshi-manitu innushkueu/I am a Damn Savage, Tanite nene etutamin nitassi?/What Have You Done to My Country?*, trans. Sarah Henzi (Waterloo: Wilfrid Laurier University Press, 2020 [1976 and 1979]).

19 [Translation] Chantal Guy, "Séquelles coloniales," *La Presse*, 20 June 2021. Guy identifies with a generation she describes as ready to make connections between "Kamloops, the relations between police and Indigenous peoples at Val-d'Or, the Viens Commission report, the death of Joyce Echaquan at the Joliette hospital, [and] the Plan Nord." [Translation] See https://www.lapresse.ca/arts/chroniques/2021-06-20/litterature/sequelles-coloniales.php.

20 [Translation] Jean-François Chassay, "L'histoire est-elle monotone?," *Voix et Images* 39, no. 3 (2014): 18. Chassay observes that the impetus for renewal "does not consist of a school or a carefully orchestrated literary movement. On the contrary: the dynamism of the writing comes from the variety of aesthetics and perspectives."

21 Laura-Julie Perreault, "Qui a peur des woke?," *La Presse*, 28 February 2021.

https://www.lapresse.ca/debats/editoriaux/2021-02-28/qui-a-peur-des-woke.php. The constituency of this "new left," and the extent to which its institutionalized representation as a political party is ready to take seriously the sovereignty of Indigenous peoples as well as anti-racist critique that may cut close to home, is a matter of debate. Québec solidaire, the democratic socialist and sovereigntist political party formed in 2006 as an alternative to the Parti Québécois's embrace of free-market principles, has taken steps to articulate a version of *indépendance* that respects the autonomy of Indigenous nations, notably committing to adoption of the United Nations Declaration on the Rights of Indigenous Peoples in its 2019 program. A militant group within the party, the Collectif anti-racist decolonial, was officially reprimanded by the party's executive committee in May 2021 for fomenting internal division. See https://www.ledevoir.com/politique/quebec/601739/conflit-a-quebec-solidaire-manon-masse-confiante.

22 Dorais, "Rompre avec le colonialisme?," 58. See also Andre Binette, "Qui aime bien, Châtie bien," *L'Aut'journal*, 17 March 2021. https://lautjournal.info/2021 0317/qui-aime-bien-chatie-bien. Binette, a specialist in constitutional and Aboriginal law in Quebec, suggests that alliance with Indigenous peoples will first require amendments to the Civil Code to reflect ancestral rights and treaties, and revenue sharing on the part of the "Hydro-Québec state" with the Innu, upon whose unceded territory the Manic-5 dam has been constructed. [Translation]

23 "Sainte-Barbe" was also used to refer to the space on the ship in which artillery-men slept and in which artillery and gun powder were stored. Saint Barbara is a martyr of the early church, invoked in thunderstorms, and the patron saint of artillery men. "Sainte-Barbe" is also the name of a municipality on the upper Saint Lawrence River and a town in the northeast of France. It also may recall another coast named by Europeans, the Barbary Coast of North Africa (from the Latin *barbaria*, "land of barbarians," foreigners – eventually meaning non-Christians).

24 Vallières' 1967 book is entitled *[N—] blancs d'Amérique: Autobiographie précoce d'un "terroriste" Québécois*. The 1971 English translation of Vallières' book put the English slur in the place of the equally racist French N-word. For Giroux's argument that not just the specific analogy drawn by Vallières, but also the wider imperial North American vernacular that functions to naturalize white entitlement, should be critically examined for what it illuminates,

and rejected, see her "N**** blanc: Essai de tout dire, ou l' autre crise
   d'Octobre," *Spirale* 277 (2021): 10–15.

25 Giroux, "Correspondences," *I Confess*, 139. *I Confess* is the text of an experimental film of the same name by the New York–based Canadian artist Moyra
   Davey that reflects on her Catholic childhood in FLQ-era Montreal and,
   through a set of memory traces and textual correspondences, on different
   valences of abjection. Giroux is an interlocutor in the film and contributes an
   essay to the accompanying book. Giroux recognizes that, in the context of
   Davey's film, and as a white Québécoise who writes from the experience of
   poverty, a "pauper who philosophizes," she is positioned as the possible "heir
   to Vallières." Giroux, "Correspondences," 139, 145.

26 [Translation] Giroux, "Correspondences," 145.

27 Giroux uses the term "psychopolitique" to describe the condition referred
   to here in a more extended phrasing. In translating her expression, I prefer
   "socio-psychic" to the possibly more familiar construction, "psycho-social."
   The latter comes from the discipline of social psychology, which is very different from the more poetic vein of social and cultural theory Giroux works
   within, one which is loosely informed by the Freudian theory of the unconscious and the Freudian use of "psychic" to mean affective energy.

28 Andrea Kunard translates *mauvais pauvre* as "bad pauper." Giroux, "Correspondences," 139.

29 The *mauvais pauvre* is the subject of a 1938 journal entry by Saint-Denys Garneau entitled, "Le mauvais pauvre va parmi nous avec son regard en dessous."
   The entry follows one that ends with a comment on the inadequacy and su-
   perficiality of nationalist struggle in the face of human suffering. Saint-Denys
   Garneau's *mauvais pauvre* is the threatening stranger, the servile and envious
   other, pitiable but repellant. Constitutionally empty, with no value of his own
   to exchange, he is described by Saint-Denys Garneau as both "*irrémédiable*"
   and "*irréparable*." A "he" for most of the entry, the *mauvais pauvre* shifts almost imperceptibly into a plural "you" (vous) by the end, so that Saint-Denys
   Garneau collapses the self-other distinction. See Hector Saint-Denys Garneau,
   Saint-Denys Garneau: Textes choisis et présentés par Benoit Lacroix (Montreal
   and Paris: Fides, 1956): 84–8. Giroux draws on the critic Yvon Rivard's discussion of the figure.

30 The "apocalyptic miracle of the third link" Giroux refers to is the proposed
   transportation tunnel to link the town of Lévis on the south shore of the Saint

Lawrence with the provincial capital, Quebec City, on the north side. The tunnel would supplement two already existing bridges. The Legault government announced the plan for the $10 billion tunnel in 2021, claiming it would bring economic development to the region. It has been criticized by environmentalists and anti-poverty activists.

31 Brian Dillon, writing of the essay tradition descended from Michel de Montaigne in *Essayism: On Form, Feeling, and Nonfiction* (New York: New York Review Books, 2017), 145. Dillon continues: the essay "invariably departs from the objects at hand to enter realms of speculation and even fantasy, because that is the liberty that such attention allows. We are … in the purview and power of the list, but not only that: also, a commitment to the deadpan unfolding of ordinary time and things – could you make an essay simply out of the things to hand at the moment you started to come back to life [from the 'excess of scrutiny and concentration … [the] exercise in deliberate attention' proper to the essay] – the photographs, the half-remembered images?," 144. Readers of *L'œil du maître* may be struck by Giroux's use of the list as a mode of paying attention, a way of taking a highly subjective inventory of the world from a localized place and time.

32 Jean-François Chassay, "Cérémonie de remise des prix littéraires 2021: Prix Victor-Barbeau, Académie des Lettres du Québec, 2 November 2021. Chassay continues, "it is a book – to recall Laurent Mailhot's definition of the essay – that 'opens itself, mines itself, and exposes itself, instead of simply imposing itself.'" [Translation] Chassay is a notable theorist of the essay as a Québécois literary form. https://www.youtube.com/watch?v=RkwU487ctrI&ab_channel =AcadémiedeslettresduQuébec.

33 Dorais, "Rompre avec le colonialisme?," 59.

34 John George Lambton, or Lord Durham, was a British liberal reformer whom the imperial government dispatched to the British North American colonies following the rebellions of 1837 to 1838 in Upper and Lower Canada, in order to investigate the causes of discontent. His diagnosis of French Canadian moral backwardness came with the recommendation that the "national character" of the British Empire be firmly established in the rebellious colony, in order to give the otherwise "stationary" francophone Catholics the chance at becoming something other than "labourers in the employ of English capitalists." http://faculty.marianopolis.edu/c.belanger/quebechistory/docs/durham/4.htm.

35 Ibid.

36 Himani Bannerji, "On the Dark Side of the Nation: Politics of Multicultural-
    ism and the State of 'Canada,'" *Journal of Canadian Studies* 31, no. 3 (Fall 1996):
    107, 109. See also Eva Mackey, *The House of Difference: Cultural Politics and
    National Identity in Canada* (London and New York: Routledge, 1999). Mackey
    discusses the commentaries in the English Canadian press on then premier
    Jacques Parizeau's racist evaluation of the causes of the "no" victory in the 1995
    referendum, when he pronounced that it was "money and the ethnic vote"
    that accounted for the victory, thereby "play[ing] right into the view" that
    "English Canada transcends the particularisms of francophone 'ethnic nation-
    alism' and [thereby offers] the universal model of civic nationhood." Mackey,
    House of Difference, 14, 15.

37 Brought in through an invoking of the "notwithstanding clause" in the Cana-
    dian Charter of Rights and Freedoms, which permits exceptions to the Char-
    ter, Quebec's Act respecting the laicity of the State forbids certain employees
    of the state, including teachers, police officers, and judges, from wearing reli-
    gious symbols while performing their duties and requires that the face not be
    covered in the course of receiving certain public services. The law has been
    critiqued as Islamophobic in its design and in its consequences for hijab-
    wearing Muslim women employed by the state, especially.

38 See Eric Andrew-Gee, James Keller, and Ian Bailey, "Cities Look to Join Fight
    against Quebec's Controversial Bill 21," *Globe and Mail*, 20 December 2021.

39 See Sarah Mushtaq, "The Liberal Government Must Rid the Country of
    Systemic Islamophobia," *Policy Options*, 8 November 2021. https://policy
    options.irpp.org/magazines/november-2021/the-liberal-government-must-
    rid-the-country-of-systemic-islamophobia.

40 Darryl Leroux studies this phenomenon in *Distorted Descent: White Claims
    to Indigenous Identity* (Winnipeg: University of Manitoba Press, 2019).

41 Giroux traces these to the Royal Proclamation of 1763, which addressed the
    troublingly dispersed geography of francophone Catholics in North America
    by creating an enclave, the "Province of Quebec," within which they would
    be enframed. At the same time, the Proclamation marked out an "Indian Re-
    serve" west of the Appalachian Mountains (again, a contiguity rather than an
    identity is what Giroux sees here: the designation of the "Indian Reserve" was
    intended to shift the movement of American settlers northward, to submerge
    the francophone population), and granted a recognition of Aboriginal title

that came with a process through which Indigenous peoples could sell their lands, but only to representatives of the British monarch. See Mackey's discussion of the Royal Proclamation as an attempt to "pla[y] different populations against each other in the interests of the British colonial project" in *House of Difference*, 27.

42 Peter Linebaugh and Marcus Rediker use these expressions for the motley social class that "undertook the labors of expropriation" in North America and the Caribbean in *The Many-Headed Hydra: Sailors, Slavers, Commoners, and the Hidden History of the Revolutionary Atlantic* (Boston: Beacon Press, 2000), 43.

43 On the list as a strategy of the essayist, see note 31, on Dillon, *Essayism*, 145.

44 *Delgamuukw v. British Columbia*, [1997] 3 S.C.R. 1010, para. 165.

INTRODUCTION

1 Just two years into a mandate, the Liberal provincial government of Premier Jean Lesage successfully ran on a single-issue platform of nationalizing the electrical industry.—Trans.

2 The Quiet Revolution refers to the period of reforms in Quebec during the 1960s. The Liberal provincial government elected in 1960 targeted patronage in politics and the control of the Catholic Church over health, social services, and education; improved the electoral representation of urban areas and strengthened state powers of regulation in relation to industry; and nationalized hydroelectric companies as part of a wider agenda of economic nationalism and secularization.—Trans.

3 Anti-racist organizer, journalist, and scholar, Emilie Nicolas, writing in French, here cites (with critical intent) the phrase used in the title of Pierre Vallières' 1967 book *[N—] blancs d'Amérique: Autobiographie précoce d'un "terroriste" Québécois*, a phrase through which Vallières appropriated the reference to chattel slavery and anti-Black racism in order to name French Canadian socio-economic abjection in the context of British-Canadian domination.—Trans.

4 [Translation] Emilie Nicolas, "Maîtres chez l'autre," *Liberté* 326 (2020), 45.

5 Giroux refers here to the critical practice of collecting and juxtaposing cultural fragments in order to expose their ideological bases and dislodge them

from the realm of edifying cultural materials belonging to the nationalist historian, bent on constructing a narrative of progress and destiny.—Trans.

6 Malcom Ferdinand, *A Decolonial Ecology: Thinking from the Caribbean World*, trans. Anthony Paul Smith (Polity, 2022).

7 Giroux names the state and capital as mutually reinforcing *dispositifs* in a later passage. The French word *dispositif*, meaning purview, plan, or device, has been translated as "apparatus" in its usage by Michel Foucault. Foucault uses *dispositif* as the name for a strategic, historically contingent way of seeing and doing that is made up of diverse elements, interrelated "forces" and "knowledges" (Foucault, "The Confession of the Flesh" in *Power/Knowledge: Selected Interviews and Other Writings, 1972–1977*, ed. Colin Gordon, trans. Colin Gordon et al. [New York: Pantheon, 1980], 196). A *dispositif* has shaping power over a milieu, but its effects are neither wholly determining nor predictable. A Foucauldian example is nineteenth-century imprisonment. See Foucault, "Confession of the Flesh," 194–228.—Trans.

8 [Translation] Rosa Pires, *Ne sommes-nous pas Québécoises?* (Montreal: Les Éditions du remue-ménage, 2019), 13–14.

9 Franco-British, that is to say, the regime constituted on the basis of legal, political, economic, and cultural inheritances stemming from successive French and British settler colonialisms in North America.

10 The French Canadian poet and painter Hector de Saint-Denys Garneau (1912–1943) is seen as the first modern poet of Quebec. A contributor to *La Relève*, the magazine of young Catholic intellectuals in Montreal, Saint-Denys Garneau published only one collection of verse, *Regards et jeux dans l'espace* (1937), which nevertheless exerted a profound influence on subsequent Quebec poetry through its modernist ruptures with rhyme scheme, syntactical order, and punctuation, and its exploration of artistic and spiritual themes. —Trans.

11 Insofar as this condition of poverty is irremediable for Saint-Denys Garneau, it is a psychic as well as a material condition. See Giroux's development of the concept in chapter 5, as well as the Translator's Introduction.—Trans.

CHAPTER ONE

1 [Translation] Extract from the documentary by Artur Lamothe, cited in IOC/RIO Tinto – *It's Time to Pay the Rent*, available at http://paytherent.info.

2 The Treaty of Paris concluded the Seven Years War, formally ending conflict between Britain and France over territory in North America. The Royal Proclamation of 1763 was a British imperial legal instrument designed to organize colonial territory in North America. Its measures to assimilate the French-speaking Catholic population of the former New France into British law and political and cultural institutions were accompanied by qualified recognition of Indigenous autonomy and land rights in previously unceded, unsold territory. Together, the two aspects of the Proclamation were designed to encourage the movement of American settlers northward, into the new "Province of Quebec," thereby helping to secure its future as a British colony.—Trans.

3 Lionel Groulx (1878–1967) was a nationalist historian and Roman Catholic priest, who led the Action française movement in the 1920s and published *Action nationale* in the 1940s, both of which attempted to galvanize support for the preservation of Catholicism and the French language in the face of urbanization and anglophone dominance in commerce and industry. Groulx's influential four-volume *Histoire du Canada français* was published between 1950 and 1952. He has come to be associated with a clericalist and sometimes anti-Semitic form of Quebec nationalism.—Trans.

4 See especially Sean Mills, *Une place au soleil: Haïti, les Haïtiens et le Québec* (Montreal: Mémoire d'encrier, 2016).

5 See Bruno Cornellier, "The Struggle of Others: Pierre Vallières, Québécois Settler Nationalism, and the N-Word Today," *Discourse* 39, no. 1 (2017): 31–66. See also Moyra Davey, *I Confess* (Ottawa: National Gallery of Canada; Brooklyn: Dancing Foxes Press, 2020), 67–76, on Vallières' problematic interpretation of the condition of the exploited French Canadian in relation to the enslavement of Africans in the Americas.

6 For a perspective on the activity of this minister under the Duplessis regime, see Jonathan Livernois, *La révolution dans l'ordre: Une histoire du duplessisme* (Montreal: Boréal, 2016).

7 Côte-Nord, or North Shore, is the name for a large administrative region in eastern Quebec stretching from the northern shore of the Saint Lawrence estuary and the Gulf of Saint Lawrence northward to an eastern boundary bordering Labrador. The region includes the traditional territory of the Innu (called Nitassinan in the Innu language) and part of the traditional territory of the Naskapi (called St'aschinuw).—Trans.

8 [Translation] Stéphane Savard, "Concilier l'exploitation hydroélectrique et la
   protection du territoire: Le cas de la Direction de l'envrionnement d'Hydro-
   Québec, 1970–1980," in Harold Bérubé and Stéphane Savard, *Pouvoir et territoire au Québec depuis 1850* (Quebec: Éditions du Septentrion, 2017), 310–11.

9 Maurice Le Noblet Duplessis (1890–1959) was the Union Nationale premier
   of Quebec from 1936 to 1939 and 1944 to 1959. His governments reinforced the
   power of the Catholic Church and industry, and worked to suppress the percolating influences of liberalism, securalism, feminism, leftist nationalism,
   and labour organizing in a conservative, rural society, earning his regime's
   era the title la Grande Noirceur, or the Great Darkness.—Trans.

10 Jean Lesage (1912–1980) was the Liberal premier of Quebec from 1960 to 1966
   and the originator of the slogan, "*Maîtres chez nous.*" His government insti-
   gated the securalizing reforms associated with the Quiet Revolution and promoted the understanding of Quebec as a state in its own right.—Trans.

11 A former Radio-Canada journalist, René Lévesque (1922–1987) took the Parti
   Québécois to a landslide victory and served two consecutive terms as premier,
   from 1976 to 1985. His governments described themselves as social democratic
   and sovereigntist: responding to union and feminist activism, they passed legislation to prohibit strikebreaking and they made Quebec the first province to
   publicly fund abortions. They enshrined French as the common public language in Quebec through Bill 101. Under Lévesque, Quebec held the first referendum on the plan to pursue the form of political independence known as
   sovereignty-association, and pressed for veto power for Quebec in negotiations on the repatriation and amendment of the Constitution, ultimately
   refusing to sign the accord.—Trans.

12 Daniel Johnson Sr. (1915–1968) was the Union nationale MLA for the district of
   Bagot for four terms; he was elected party leader in 1961 and became premier
   when the party won the 1966 election under the slogan "*égalité ou indépendance,*" also the title of his 1965 book. As minister of hydraulic resources in
   1960, Johnson initiated a multi-dam hydro-electrical development on the
   Manicouagan and Outardes rivers.—Trans.

13 A lawyer and economist, Robert Bourassa (1933–1996) was the Liberal premier
   of Quebec from 1970 to 1976 and again from 1985 to 1994, governing during
   the October Crisis of 1970 (and famously requesting that the prime minister
   invoke the War Measures Act) and the federal government's announcement
   of its policy of multiculturalism (which the Bourassa government opposed

on the grounds that it disconnected culture from language), and initiating the James Bay hydroelectric project in 1971, without undertaking consultations with the Cree and Inuit of northern Quebec until forced to do so by a court injunction.—Trans.

14 An economist, Bernard Landry was the premier of Quebec in 2001 to 2003 and led the Parti Québécois until 2005. Following decades of Cree struggle to insist that Quebec uphold its obligations to share revenue and jointly manage natural resources industries in Eeyou Istchee, their traditional lands in northern Quebec, according to the terms of the 1975 James Bay Agreement, the Landry government signed the Agreement Respecting a new Relationship Between the Cree Nation and the Government of Quebec, or La Paix des Braves, in 2002. While this agreement provides for Cree participation in and some measure of control over the development of ancestral lands, it has been seen as a tool of "institutional reconciliation," serving to integrate the Cree into Quebec society by implanting bureaucratic forms of government as well as settler legal and political categories. See Frédérique Dombrowski, "The *Paix des Braves*: A Path Toward Reconciliation?" (Master's thesis, York University, 2016).—Trans.

15 Jean Charest became the first French Canadian leader of the federal Conservative Party in 1993, and during the 1995 referendum over sovereignty in Quebec argued that Quebec should pursue its interests within Canada rather than seek separation. He resigned as the federal Conservative leader in 1998 and assumed the leadership of the Liberal Party in Quebec, forming a government after defeating the Parti Québécois in the 2003 election. Charest won three successive mandates and, under the slogan "*L'économie, d'abord, oui*" (Yes to the economy, first), presided over a series of neoliberal reforms that included privatization of certain industries and substantial increases to university tuition fees.—Trans.

16 Launched by the Liberal government of Jean Charest in 2011, the Plan Nord refers to a twenty-five-year public-private investment plan for the development of natural resources, especially minerals mining, in Quebec north of the Saint Lawrence River and the Gulf of Saint Lawrence. While the plan was promoted as representing a shared vision for sustainable development, it has been criticized for dealing with affected Indigenous communities individually in such a way as to bypass nation-to-nation negotiations, and for prioritizing government partnerships with resource extraction multinationals, sidelining local community interests.—Trans.

17 The British-Canadian law that fixed the limits of the "Province of Quebec" at
the turn of the twentieth century, the Quebec Boundaries Extension Act, 1912,
explicitly stated that Quebec would be obliged (and accredited) to pursue federal native land title cessation practices in relation to Indigenous territory. Ar-
ticle 2 of the 1912 law stipulates "c) That the province of Quebec will recognize
the rights of the Indian inhabitants in the territory above described to the
same extent, and will obtain surrenders of such rights in the same manner,
as the Government of Canada has heretofore recognized such rights and has
obtained surrender thereof, and the said province shall bear and satisfy all
charges and expenditure in connection with or arising out of such surrenders;
d) That no such surrender shall be made or obtained except with the approval
of the Governor in Council; e) That the trusteeship of the Indians in the said
territory, and the management of any lands now or hereafter reserved for their
use, shall remain in the Government of Canada subject to the control of Parliament." British North America Acts, 1867-1907; Together with Other Imperial
Statues Relating to Canada; Imperial Order-in-Council Admitting Ruperts
Land, British Columbia, and Prince Edward Island, Respectively into the
Union; the Manitoba, Alberta, Saskatchewan, Northwest Territories and
Yukon Acts (Canada) with Various Amending Acts; and Other Canadian
Statues Relating to the Provincial Subsidies and to the Boundaries of the
Provinces Down to 1912 (Ottawa: King's Printer, 1913), 236.
18 [Translation] Caroline Desbien, *Puissance Nord, Territoire, identité et culture
de l'hydroélecricité au Québec* (Sainte-Foye: Laval University Press, 2014), 9.
19 [Translation] Zebedee Nungak, *Contre le colonialism dopé aux stéroïdes: Le
combat des Inuits du Québec pour leur terres ancestrales* (Montreal: Boréal,
2019), 42.
20 On the question of the Act respecting the laicity of the State, see Dalie Giroux,
"La question nationale et de la laïcité au Québec: Psychopolitique d'une intri-
cation," in *Modération ou extrémisme? Regards critiques sur la loi 21*, ed. L.
Ceilis et al., (Quebec: University of Quebec Press, 2020) 13–28. On the Wet'-
suwet'en issue, see Giroux, "Nation Wet'suwet'en: Non au colonialisme, au
capitalisme et à l'extractivisme" at https://alter.quebec/nation-wetsuweten-
non-au-colonialisme-au-capitalisme-et-a-lextractivisme.
21 Giroux writes "epistemic murk" in italicized English. See Michael Taussig,
"Culture of Terror – Space of Death: Roger Casement's Putumayo Report and
the Explanation of Torture," *Comparative Studies in Society and History* 26,

no. 3 (1984): 492. The Marxist cultural anthropologist uses the expression to
refer to the effect of colonial representation "creating an uncertain … night-
marish reality in which the unstable interplay of truth and illusion becomes
a social force of horrendous and phantasmic dimensions" affecting both
colonized and colonizer.—Trans.

22 See for example *Delgamuukw v. British Columbia*, [1997] 3 S.C.R. 1010, para.
165: "the range of legislative objectives that can justify the infringement of
Aboriginal title is fairly broad. Most of these objectives can be traced to the
reconciliation of the prior occupation of North America by Aboriginal peoples
with the assertion of Crown sovereignty, which entails the recognition that
'distinctive Aboriginal societies exist within, and are a part of, a broader social,
political and economic community' (at para. 73). In my opinion, the development of agriculture, forestry, mining, and hydroelectric power, the general
economic development of the interior of British Columbia, protection of the
environment or endangered species, *the building of infrastructure and the settlement of foreign populations to support those aims*, are the kinds of objectives
that are consistent with this purpose" [emphasis added by author].

23 See Peter N. Moogk, "Reluctant Exiles: Emigrants from France in Canada before 1760," *William and Mary Quarterly* 46, no. 3 (1989). Moogk provides a de-
mographic and historical demonstration of his thesis that French immigrants
in New France were for the most part temporary migrant workers (and included hired men, soldiers, *filles du roi*, and slaves), who did not intend to
establish themselves as colonists in New France.

24 "*Alouette*" is used to signify "etc." or "and the list could go on and on," as
Giroux plays on the French-language children's song of that name (a song
thought to be of French Canadian origin) through which many preschool
children have learned to name body parts.—Trans.

25 [Translation] "L'égalitarisme paysan dans l'ancienne société rurale de la vallée
du Saint-Laurent: Élements pour une réinterprétation," *Le monde rural
Québécois aux XVIIIe et XIXe siècles: Cultures, hiérarchies, pouvoirs* (Montreal:
Fides, 2018), 197.

26 These canonical perspectives were disseminated through the works of
François-Xavier Garneau, right up to those of Marcel Trudel; they were force-
fully questioned by Louise Dechêne and Christian Dessureault beginning in
the 1970s. The vision of New France as a cocoon nevertheless persists, like a
prejudice, and nourishes the idea – forceful, but neither true nor false – that

the colony was violently destroyed by the British in 1759 and by its successive abandonments by France, thereby marking a before and after of French life in the Americas. In fact, numerous works point to a deterioration in conditions on the *seigneuries*, especially from 1815 on, for a number of reasons but the most likely being an accelerated transition to a capitalist mode of production. See Christian Dessureault, "L'évolution du régime seigneurial Canadien de 1760 à 1854: Essai de synthèse," *Le monde rural Québécois aux XVIIIe et XIXe siècles*, 135–60.

27 Note that the official documents attesting to this transfer do not even mention the animals and plants that were part of the territory. A whole subaltern world thereby is confirmed in its status of a nature that simply awaits appropriation. The colonial hierarchy positions humans at the top of a grand scheme to capture and accumulate, and places the ensemble of the living, animate world at the very bottom of the scale.

28 Quebec became a province within the Canadian federation, having its own provincial government, as part of Confederation in 1867. Previously, when first absorbed into the British Empire, it had been known as the "Province of Quebec" (from 1763–91); later it was known as Lower Canada (1791–1841) and then Canada East (1841–67).—Trans.

29 Jacques Ferron (1921–1985) was a physician; socialist; writer of plays, short fiction, and novels; founder of the Rhinoceros Party; mediator for the Front de libération du Québec in the context of the October Crisis; and candidate for the Cooperative Commonwealth Federation (precursor to the New Democratic Party) in the 1956 federal election. He wrote fables, social satires, allegories, innovative treatments of history, and political and philosophical essays. *Contes du pays incertain* (translated as *Tales from the Uncertain Country* in 1972) won the Governor General's Award for fiction in 1962.—Trans.

30 Adam Dollard des Ormeaux (1635–1660) was the garrison commander of the fort of Ville-Marie (now Montreal). He died in the Battle of Long Sault where, with Huron and Algonquin allies, he is believed to have been attempting to ward off an Iroquois war party headed east. In Quebec he is commemorated through the naming of streets, public squares, parks, and a Montreal suburb.—Trans.

31 [Translation] Ferron names the two Quebec-based banking institutions in order to evoke a more materialist record of the people. Claims to cultural particularity and authenticity are grounded, ultimately, in savings built up locally,

and as Giroux stresses, in a state power indissociable from Indigenous dispossession and natural resource extraction. The Montreal-based Banque
d'Hochelaga was founded in 1874. The first Caisse Populaire Desjardins,
a credit union, was founded in Lévis in 1990.—Trans.

32 The Patriotes was a francophone political party as well as a broader, liberal,
and nationalist political movement of the late 1820s and 1830s in Lower
Canada. The Patriotes dominated the elected House of Assembly but con-
tended with an appointed Legislative Council held by British colonial administrators, members of the aristocracy, and an anglophone merchant class. In
the revolts of 1837 and 1838, militants took up arms to respond to Britain's
rejection of the Assembly's demand for more democratic government as well
as its dispatching of troops to the colony to repress growing unrest.—Trans.

33 The Front de libération du Québec was a militant movement for Quebec in-
dependence influenced by anti-colonial, socialist revolutions in Algeria and
Cuba, and making use of the memory and symbols of the nineteenth-century
Patriotes. Active from 1963 to 1970, especially in cells operating in Montreal,
the FLQ's activities culminated in what came to be called the
October Crisis.—Trans.

34 [Translation] Cited with emphasis in Harold Bérubé and Stéphane Savard,
Pouvoir et territoire au Québec depuis 1850 (Quebec: Éditions du Septentrion,
2017).

35 *Pharmakon*, a word in ancient Greek, is used for both remedy and poison – for
illness, for the cause of the illness, or for the cure. Jacques Derrida traces the
ambivalence of the term through Plato's dialogues, stressing its association
with writing in "Phaedrus." See Jacques Derrida, "Plato's Pharmacy," *Dissemi-
nation*, trans. Barbara Johnson (Chicago: University of Chicago Press, 1972).
—Trans.

36 François Legault, a former Parti Québécois cabinet minister, founded Coalition Avenir Québec in 2012 along with the businessman Charles Sirois.

37 [Translation] Emilie Nicolas, "Maîtres chez l'autre," 44.

38 Giroux borrows this phrase from the Supreme Court decision in *Tsilhqot'in
Nation v. British Columbia*, 2014 SCC 44, [2014] 2 S.C.R. 256, which recalls
the justifiable grounds for incursions on Aboriginal title lands established in
section 35 of the Constitution Act, 1982.—Trans.

39 The 1975 James Bay and Northern Quebec Agreement is the first modern comprehensive land claim agreement in Canada. Following large-scale hydroelec-

tric development in the unceded land of Eeyou Istchee, launched in 1971 as the
first undertaking of the new James Bay Development Corporation – without
consultation with either the James Bay Cree or the Inuit of the region, the
Quebec Association of Indians sued the provincial government and won a
legal requirement that a treaty be negotiated. Under the 1975 Agreement,
Cree land title was extinguished in exchange for recognition of specific Cree
and Inuit rights and monetary compensation of $225 million over twenty
years.—Trans.

40 [Translation] Jean-Jacques Simard, "Développement et government autochtones: L'expérience de la baie James et du Nord Québécois," *Politiques
et Sociétés* 28 (1995): 85.

41 "Roxham Road" refers to a rural road that serves as an unauthorized land border crossing between Canada and the US, south of Montreal and north of
Plattsburgh, New York. Especially between 2017 and 2020, thousands of racialized asylum seekers leaving the US due to the threat of deportation in the
context of the Trump administration's tighter restrictions on immigration,
entered Canada through Roxham Road. They used the unofficial crossing in
order to avoid being immediately returned by Canada to the US under the
terms of a 2004 treaty, the Safe Third Country Agreement, which applies to official ports of entry only. At unofficial entries such as Roxham Road they can
begin the process of applying for asylum – a step toward refugee status – once
they have crossed the border (and often having been apprehended by the
RCMP). In offering Roxham Road as a figure for the openings to be found
within the settler-colonial capitalist state structure, Giroux stresses that decolonization involves active solidarity with those subject to state border controls
and regulation of "legal" and "illegal" statuses.—Trans.

42 Giroux understands the "Franco-British colonial territories" she refers to here
as territories organized by a global neoliberal capitalist circulation machine.
In her *La généalogie du déracinement* (Montreal: University of Montreal Press,
2019), she calls for alternative forms of inhabitation and circulation rooted in
Indigenous knowledge and history, as well as in a determination to remain in
place, which is not, as the capitalist circulation machine would have it, equivalent to death, but a practice of intensive local engagement, a bricolage of tools,
actions, and alliances for countering human alienation and dispossession, as
well as the destruction of non-human nature.—Trans.

CHAPTER TWO

1 Rémi Savard, *Destins d'Amérique: Les Autochtones et nous* (Montreal: L'Hexagone, 1979), 26.

2 Sean Mills, *The Empire Within: Postcolonial Thought and Political Activism in Sixties Montreal* (Montreal and Kingston: McGill-Queen's University Press, 2010), 60. [The author cites from the French translation of Mills' text, *Contester l'empire: Pensée postcoloniale et militantisme politique à Montréal, 1963–1972* (Montreal: Hurtubise, 2011), 81.—Trans.]

3 Jacques Godbout is a Québécois poet, novelist, essayist, and documentary filmmaker whose major works appeared in the 1960s, 1970s, and 1908s. His fiction is known for its satirical and sometimes allegorical treatments of Quebec's relation to English-speaking North America, including a puritanical English Canada and a hyper-consumerist United States.—Trans.

4 On the contemporary claiming of Métis identity in Quebec, see chapters 4 and 5 of Darryl Leroux, *Distorted Descent: White Claims to Indigenous Identity* (Winnipeg: University of Manitoba Press, 2019).

5 An autodidact, Raoul Roy was an advocate of socialist decolonization for Quebec on the models of Cuba and Algeria. He founded the *Revue socialiste* in 1959. As Sean Mills observes, Roy's politics were contradictory: while he called for "solidarity with all oppressed groups in North America," he saw immigration as part of a plot of the imperial bourgeoisie. Mills, *The Empire Within*, 42.—Trans.

6 André Major is a poet, a writer of short fiction, and novels, notably the trilogy *Histoires des déserteurs*, depicting a violent rural Quebec. In the early 1960s, Major was a contributor to the influential Montreal-based cultural and political journal *Parti pris*, before shifting course and becoming a literary editor of the Catholic, nationalist publication *L'Action nationale*.—Trans.

7 Vallières' book was translated as *Choose!* (Toronto: New Press, 1972).—Trans.

8 The Mouvement de libération populaire was a political party committed to socialist revolution and Quebec independence. Its manifesto, published in 1965 in the journal *Parti pris*, provided an analysis of the Québécois working class as being caught between a new domestic bourgeoisie, American capitalism, and the Canadian federal state acting as the latter's agent. See Mills, *The Empire Within*, 57.—Trans.

9   [Translation] Daniel Samson-Legault, *Dissident: Pierre Vallières (1938–1998) –*
    Au-delà de [N—] blancs d'Amérique (Montreal: Québec-Amérique, 2018), 391.
10 Ibid.
11 Mills, *The Empire Within*, 61.
12 *Felquiste* refers to an FLQ-ist, that is, a supporter of the Front de libération du
    Québec.—Trans.
13 Born into a very large, poor family in the Quebec village of Le Bic, Charles
    Gagnon (1939–2005) founded the Marxist and anti-colonial Québécois journal
    Révolution Québécoise with Pierre Vallières in 1964. The journal linked the
    struggle for national liberation in Québéc to struggles in the Third World and
    attempted to bring the ideas of Black liberation to its francophone Québécois
    audience. In 1967 Gagnon wrote *Feu sur l'Amérique: Une proposition pour la*
    révolution nord-américaine while in prison. Gagnon was a leading member of
    the FLQ, and in the 1970s of the Maoist organization En Lutte!—Trans.
14 [Translation] Charles Gagnon, *Feu sur l'Amérique: Écrits volumes 1, 1966–1972*
    (Montreal: Lux Éditeur, 2006), 117.
15 Gagnon, *Feu sur l'Amérique*, 78.
16 Jean Morisset is a poet, essayist, and geographer, born in the municipality of
    Bellechasse, east of Quebec City on the south shore of the Saint Lawrence
    River. In addition to documenting Dene experience of colonialism in the
    North in the context of the Mackenzie Valley Pipeline project, Morisset's re-
    search and writing has described the multiplicity and variety of francophone
    North America and explored Quebec's relationship to Haiti. Morisset taught
    in the Department of Geography at the Université du Québec à Montréal.
    —Trans.
17 First published in 1977 and re-issued in 2009 by Mémoire d'encrier.
18 The critique may be found in "Québec, Baie-James et Premières Nations: Our
    la décolonisation assujettie," *Nouveaux cahiers du socialisme*, 18 (2017). Along-
    side this critique should be read the passionate interventions of the sociologist
    Jean-Jacques Simard on the same question. I have not been able to find these
    in Simard's published texts, but Rémi Savard recalled his key points in an in-
    terview: "[Simard] applied the model of the James Bay Agreement to an agree-
    ment between Quebec and Ottawa … First, all of Quebec would be given to
    Ottawa (cessation of title); in return, we would obtain category 1 lands around
    our main cities, minus any property rights in their natural resources; as well,

we would be allocated several category 2 lands, in which we would have the right to practice our traditional activities (law and medicine, bingo, dancing, singing, etc.); all of the rest would become Crown land and would belong to the federal government" (Savard, *Destins d'Amerique*, 173–4). [Translation]

19 The title translates as "The New Quebec: Or, how the colonized treat their colony." The report was produced by the Centrale de l'enseignement du Québec.—Trans.

20 Mills, *The Empire Within*, 213.

21 Howard Adams, *Prison of Grass: Canada from a Native Point of View* (Saskatoon: Fifth House, 1989), 181–2. Born in Saskatchewan, Howard Adams (1921–2001) was an important Métis writer, orator, educator, and activist. *Prison of Grass*, first published in 1975, is an analysis of colonialism and racism in Canada; a later work, *Tortured People: The Politics of Colonization* (1995), extended the earlier analysis to encompass the problem of neo-colonialism among Indigenous leaders. Adams taught at the University of Saskatchewan and the University of California. While completing his doctorate at the latter in the 1960s, he was influenced by the ideas of Black liberation.—Trans.

22 The Laboratoire d'anthropologie amérindienne was an autonomous research group founded in 1970 and led by Rémi Savard, professor of anthropology at Laval University and then the University of Montreal. The research of its members – including Sylvie Vincent, Innu poet Joséphine Bacon, José Mailhot, Madeleine Lefebvre, and Claude Lachapelle – established the field of Québécois anthropology centred on Indigenous peoples of the Americas and especially the Innu of the Côte Nord and Labrador.—Trans.

23 The work of the film director Arthur Lamothe is equally important to signal in this context. Lamothe, with the help of Thérèse Rock as translator, contributed to the documentation of Innu life, often working alongside the anthropologist Rémi Savard.

24 One should also mention the late 1970s collaboration between Rémi Savard and the Ligue des droits de l'homme (precursor to the Ligue des droits et liberté du Québec) in bringing to light the colonial violence perpetrated during an episode of the salmon war between the Innu and the Quebec government on the Moisie River (notably the suspicious circumstances surrounding the deaths of Achille Vollant and Moïse Régis in 1977). For more detail, including the disappointing verdict of the 1998 Roberge Commission, see Amélie-Anne

Mailhot, "'L'art pour manger': Explorations du complexe de l'autonomie ali-
mentaire innue comme mémoire de liberté politique dans les lieux de friction
des habitations politiques du Nitassinan" (doctoral thesis, University of
Ottawa 2019), 210–11.

25 [Translation] Savard, *Destins d'Amerique*, 152.

26 [Translation] Ibid., 26.

27 In the process, Quebec threw overboard the whole of francophone Canada,
which, from the point of view of Quebec was, like Indigenous peoples, in the
process of extinction.

28 [Translation] Savard, *Destins d'Amerique*, 181.

29 In response to growing nationalist sentiment and separatist aspirations in
Quebec in the context of the Quiet Revolution, the federal government estab-
lished the Royal Commission on Bilingualism and Biculturalism (1963–9). The
Commission found that francophones faced inequities in a number of sectors.
The hope was that Commission recommendations for partnership between
Canada's so-called "founding peoples" would dampen discontent. One of the
Commission's recommendations was for English and French to be made the
official languages of Canada. The Official Languages Act was passed in 1969.
—Trans.

30 [Translation] Savard, *Destins d'Amerique*, 40.

31 In 1995, Pierre Trudel wrote that such theories are the most common form
of negation of Indigenous identity within the Québécois political class. See
Pierre Trudel, "De la négation de l'Autre dans les discours nationalistes des
Québécois et des Autochtones," *Recherches amérindiennes au Québec* 25, no. 4
(1995): 59, in which Trudel writes: "And if there is a crisis, [there is] no point
examining the governing practices of Quebec or its position on the recognition of the Indigenous peoples' right of self-determination: instead, we'll
unmask the federalist plot."

32 The 1969 White Paper was a policy paper of the Liberal government of Prime
Minister Pierre Trudeau. It proposed to unilaterally abolish the Indian Act,
thereby ending the special legal relationship between Indigenous peoples and
the Canadian state, and terminating "Indian" as a legal status. Adoption of the
policy would have meant the transferal of reserve land to individual property
owners and the management of any remaining relationship to government at
the level of the provinces. The rationale for the proposal was that Indigenous

peoples should be treated "equally" with Canadian citizens. Indigenous organizations mounted a powerful resistance to the proposal, pointing to the
federal government's responsibility to honour treaty obligations.—Trans.

33 The Assembly of First Nations grew out of the National Indian Brotherhood
    (NIB), which itself emerged from an earlier group of organizations, some
    reaching back to the first quarter of the twentieth century. An organization
    contemporaneous with the NIB, the North American Indian Nation Govern-
    ment, which defended Indigenous rights on the American continent, was
    founded in 1945 by Jules Sioui, from Wendake, near Quebec; William Com-
    manda, from Kitigan Zibi in the Gatineau River valley, was its supreme chief
    in this era. This is to say that Indigenous resistance is ancient on this conti-
    nent, it totally escapes institutional power, and it has its bases in Quebec as
    much as in Western Canada. Let us recall that *Akwesasne Notes*, literary beacon
    of Red Power during the 1960s, was printed and published in the Québécois
    part of the Akwesasne reserve.

34 Savard, *Destins d'Amerique*, 36.

35 On the history of the numbered treaties, see Olive P. Dickason, *Canada's First
    Nations: A History of Founding Peoples* (Toronto: McClelland & Stewart, 1992).

36 On the regional aspect of anti-Indigenous racism in Quebec, see Audrey Lord,
    *L'approche commune: Nouvelle Alliance innue-Québécoise – La réaction au
    Saguenay-Lac-Saint-Jean, 2000–2004* (Université du Québec à Chicoutimi:
    GRIR éditeur, 2010); Brieg Capitaine, "Expressions ordinaires et politiques du
    racism anti-authochtone au Quebec," *Sociologie et Sociétés*, 50, no. 2 (2018):
    77–99; Leroux, *Distorted Descent*.

37 For a very rich study of the difference between Indigenous and colonial con-
    ceptions of territory, see Julie Depelteau, *Nitaskinan, territoire: Analyse des
    discours des représentatnts politiques des Atikamekws Nehirowisiwok at des
    gouvernements coloniaux, 1973–2004* (doctoral dissertation, University of
    Ottawa, 2019).

38 Giroux here uses the English expression for those who carry or bring water,
    in order to signify a social category of menial labourers.—Trans.

39 *Péquiste* refers to a PQ-ist, that is, a supporter of the Parti Québécois.—Trans.

40 [Translation] Savard, *Destins d'Amerique*, 109.

41 *Domaine* in the original. Thanks to Bruce Curtis and John Manwaring for
    advice on legal terminology in this paragraph.—Trans.

42 The British North America Act is the agreement passed by the British Parlia-

ment in 1867, through which the then British colonies of Ontario, Quebec, Nova Scotia, and New Brunswick were combined into a federated union, becoming the provinces of Canada. The Act describes a parliamentary system on the model of the British one and lays out the jurisdiction and powers of the federal government and the provincial legislatures, with the former retaining substantial centralized powers. Until 1982, amendments to the constitution were under British jurisdiction.—Trans.

43 The seigneurial system was a form of semi-feudal land occupation and distribution in New France through which members of the colonial elite (colonial administrators, military officers, members of the nobility, and the church) were granted ownership of large parcels of land along the banks of the Saint Lawrence River and they, in turn, granted tenancies to farmers (called *habitants*) who paid annual rents, taxes on their crops, and worked a certain number of days per year for the *seigneur*. The system was officially abolished in 1854 but the payment of an annual rent to the landowner continued until 1935, and then in a qualified way until 1970.—Trans.

44 Gérald Godin (1938–94) was a poet, journalist, and Parti Québécois politician who represented the Montreal riding of Mercier from 1976 to 1994. Godin's poetry became overtly political with the collection *Les Cantouques*, published in 1967. He and his partner, the singer Pauline Julien, were among those arrested and detained for suspected terrorism and connections to the FLQ in 1970 under the War Measures Act.—Trans.

45 Savard, *Destins d'Amerique*, 109.

46 Ibid., 110.

47 Ibid., 178.

48 The Great Peace of Montreal was an agreement reached in 1701 between the French and the Five Nations of the Haudenosaunee. The agreement involved thirty-nine nations from northeastern North America in a peace treaty with the French, and was achieved through ceremonies centred on Haudenosaunee diplomatic protocols. In the previous century, Samuel de Champlain had allied the French with the Algonquin Anishinaabeg and the Huron-Wendat, thereby positioning the French against the Haudenosaunee, the Indigenous allies of the English.—Trans.

49 Savard, *Destins d'Amerique*, 179.

50 Ibid., 180.

51 On whiteness as a political category in the context of Indigenous studies, see

Aileen Moreton-Robinson, *White Possessive: Property, Power, and Indigenous Sovereignty* (Minneapolis: University of Minnesota Press, 2015); and Amélie-Anne Mailhot, "La perspective de l'habitation politique dans *Je suis une maudite sauvagesse/Eukuan nin matshimanitu innu-iskueu* by An Antane Kapesh," *Recherches féministes* 30, no. 1 (2017): 29–45.

52 [Translation] Edgard Rochette, *Notes sur la Côte Nord du Bas Saint-Laurent et le Labrador canadien* (Quebec: Imprimerie Le Soleil, 1926). Rochette was a cabinet minister in the Liberal provincial governments of Louis-Alexandre Taschereau and Adélard Godbout in the 1930s and early 1940s, holding, in turn, the posts of minister of employment; minister of employment, hunting, and fishing; and minister of mines and fishing.—Trans.

53 Jacques Ferron, Madeleine Ferron, and Robert Cliche, *Le monde a-t-il fait la culbute? Correspondances 3, 1966–1985*, edited by Marcel Olscamp and Lucie Joubert (Montreal: Lemeac, 2019), 462.

54 It is true that in the moment of the referenda of 1908 and 1995, the Inuit and Cree organized their own referenda in order to demonstrate their opposition to the sovereignty-association project of Quebec, by a crushing majority. For a fiercely anti-Québécois perspective, see Zebedee Nungak, *Contre le colonialism dopé aux stéroïdes: Le combat des Inuits du Québec pour leur terres ancestrales* (Montreal: Boréal, 2019). For an original and interesting reading of the 1980 referendum and the Indigenous question, see Jean Morisset, "Les Autochtones et le 20 mai," *Le Devoir*, 14 May 1980, 10.

55 Noel Victor Starblanket (1946–2019) was Cree from the Starblanket reserve in Treaty 4 territory, Saskatchewan. Born in Fort Qu'Appelle, he was a residential school survivor who later attended law school at the University of Saskatchewan and was a filmmaker with the National Film Board's "Indian Film Crew." He was twice elected president of the NIB, in 1975 and 1978. In addition to extending the hand of the NIB to Lévesque in this period, Starblanket initiated a dialogue (notably, despite lack of support from the NIB executive council) with the group Indian Rights for Indian Women, which was seeking to reform gender-discriminatory sections of the Indian Act.—Trans.

56 [Translation] Savard, *Destins d'Amerique*, 177–8.

57 Section 35(1) of the Constitution Act recognizes "existing aboriginal and treaty rights." Section 25 references the "aboriginal, treaty, or other rights and freedoms" recognized in the Royal Proclamation of 1763. With the Constitution Act of 1982, authority over the Constitution was transferred from the British

parliament to Canada's federal and provincial legislatures, and a Charter of Rights and Freedoms was created. The patriation of the Constitution was preceded by complex and fractious negotiations between federal and provincial governments. Quebec did not consent to the amended terms, which were agreed upon by the other provinces in discussions that famously excluded the delegation from Quebec.—Trans.

58 George Manuel (1921–1989), OC, was an Indigenous leader and the co-author of the treatise calling for political unity of Indigenous peoples affected by colonialism, *The Fourth World: An Indian Reality* (1975). A member of the Neskonlith Band of the Shuswap Nation, Manuel was a survivor of residential school. He became president of the North American Indian Brotherhood of BC in 1959 and was later president of the NIB (1970–6) and the Union of BC Indian Chiefs (1979–81). He launched the World Council of Indigenous Peoples in 1975. Manuel organized the Constitutional Express in 1980, mobilizing demand for recognition of Aboriginal rights in the Constitution.—Trans.

59 Ian Mulgrew, "Patriation: The Next Step B.C. Indians Declare 'War' on Ottawa," *Globe and Mail*, 7 November 1981.

60 Georges Henry Erasmus, OC, is an Indigenous leader and advocate of nation-to-nation relationships. Born in 1948 in a Dene community, Behchok , in the Northwest Territories, he became president of the Dene Nation in 1974 and asserted Dene sovereignty in the face of the proposed Mackenzie Valley Pipeline in 1976. He was the national chief of the Assembly of First Nations (1985–91) and co-chair of the Royal Commission on Aboriginal Peoples (1991–1996). —Trans.

61 [Translation] Cited in Jean Morisset, *Sur la piste du Canada errant* (Montreal: Boréal, 2018), 356. Georges Erasmus spoke these words in a November 1981 interview for the Radio-Canada television programme *Présent national*. Excerpts from that interview, conducted in English, were subsequently broadcast with partial French voice-over when *Présent national* asked Morisset and the Parti Québécois minister Gérald Godin for their responses in a 12 November 1981 broadcast. Morisset quotes from his transcription of the interview and observes that Erasmus made similar statements in Ottawa on 9 and 15 November 1981. Thanks to Jean Morisset for this clarification.—Trans.

62 [Translation] Morisset, *Sur la piste du Canada errant*, 356–7. Morisset quotes from his own transcription of the interview for the Radio-Canada show. —Trans.

63 [Translation] Jean Morisset, from the unpublished original manuscript of *Sur la piste du Canada errant.*

64 See Jean Morisset's intervention on this question in "Quant le Canada triomphe des Indiens et des Québécois," *Le Devoir*, 6 January 1982.

65 [Translation] Savard, *Destins d'Amerique*, 155.

66 [Translation] Ibid., 110.

67 [Translation] Ibid., 154.

68 The author's phrase, "*chasse-galerie contre chasse-partie*," plays on similar-sounding but very distinct social positions and contexts. *Chasse-galerie* refers to the French Canadian adaptation of a French legend. In Honoré Beaugrand's influential 1892 print version of this legend, a group of lumberjacks in the Outaouais region of western Quebec make a pact with the devil in order to "run the *chasse-galerie*" or paddle home through the sky in their big canoe. Here, Giroux associates the legend's lumberjacks with the *coureurs de bois*, the unlicensed men of the fur trade. The phrase "*chasse-galerie contre chasse-partie*" underlines the contrast between these rough outlaw figures and the aristocratic hunting-party, or *chasse-partie*, of the Old World.—Trans.

69 [Translation] Jean Merrien, *Histoire mondiale des pirates, flibustiers et négriers* (Paris: Grasset, 1959), 178.

70 On the question of "epistemic displacement" in relation to Quebec and Nitassinan, see Mailhot, "'L'art pour manger,'" 210–11.

71 Giroux's "*se rencontrer dans les lieux de vie*" recalls her imagining of a way of centring ourselves locally, through practices of alliance, neighbourliness, and multidimensional political activism, against the pressures to keep moving and consuming within the circuits of global capital, in her *La généalogie du déracinement* (Montreal: University of Montreal Press, 2019).

CHAPTER THREE

1 [Translation] Jean Morisset, "Le Québec fictif et le detournement autochtone," *Le Devoir*, 13 February 1992, B10.

2 The Crown is the symbolic and ceremonial source of the sovereign authority claimed within the system of legislative, executive, and judicial powers of federal and provincial governments in Canada. The British monarch and its vice-regal representatives are its embodiment.—Trans.

3 Giroux quotes the phrase, "*chaque corps qui se déplace dans l'espace a droit a*

son utilité," from a 1968 National Film Board documentary by Pierre Perrault, *Les voitures d'eau* (*The River Schooners*), the third film in Perrault's trilogy about life in Îles-aux-Coudres, an island east of Quebec City on the Saint Lawrence. The second film in the trilogy is discussed in chapter 4.—Trans.

4 The author here lists television series broadcast by Radio-Canada, the French-language service of Canada's public broadcasting corporation. For the most part these are long-running series of the 1980s, soap operas focused on working-class family life among white, rural Québécois, some in historical settings, some adapted from novels. *Monsieur le minister* (1982–6) was a realist series dramatizing a husband and father's entry into electoral politics. *Shehaweh* (1993) was a five-episode costume drama about the adventures of an Indigenous heroine taken to France and returned to Canada as a *fille du roi*.—Trans.

5 The 1980 Quebec referendum was a direct vote held by the Parti Québécois government of René Lévesque that asked voters whether or not they supported a mandate for the government to seek a new relationship between the province and the federal government based on the idea of sovereignty-association, which would allow for political independence combined with economic association. The second referendum, in 1995, was held by the Parti Québécois government of Jacques Parizeau, and simply asked voters whether Quebec should become sovereign. Notably, the Grand Council of the Crees in Quebec and the Inuit of Nunavik held their own referenda, on Quebec separation from Canada and Quebec sovereignty, respectively.—Trans.

6 CÉGEP is an acronym for Collège d'enseignement général et professionnel. These publically funded colleges provide two years of higher education in preparation for university (and a diplôme d'études collégiales or DEC, required in addition to a secondary diploma for Quebec students entering university) or three-year technical programs preparing students for work. —Trans.

7 Lucien Bouchard was the leader of the Parti Québécois and the premier of Quebec from 1996 to 2001. He had previously served as a Progressive Conservative and then Bloc Québécois member of Parliament, having formed the latter party in 1991. Bouchard lost his left leg through a rare bacterial infection in 1994. The famous line comes from his period of hospitalization.—Trans.

8 Following the narrow defeat of the "yes" side in the October 1995 referendum, which would have affirmed a form of separation or sovereignty for Quebec, Premier Jacques Parizeau (whose nickname in the media and political circles

was *Monsieur*) famously attributed the defeat to *"l'argent puis des votes ethniques, essentiellment"* (money and the ethnic vote, essentially). https://www. ledevoir.com/politique/quebec/588468/referendum-de-1995-la-declaration-choc-decortiquee.—Trans.

9 André Boisclair was the leader of the Parti Québécois from 2005 to 2007, after serving as a cabinet minister from 1998 to 2003. He resigned as leader after the PQ fell to third place in the 2007 provincial election.—Trans.

10 Giroux refers to a 2011 internal crisis and mutiny within the Parti Québécois, when under the leadership of Pauline Marois, the minority government proposed a law to prevent legal contestation of Quebec City's partnership with the company Québecor, in the operation of an amphitheatre, the Centre Vidéotron.—Trans.

11 Economist Jean-Martin Aussant was elected a Parti Québécois member of the Quebec National Assembly in 2008, becoming an independent and then creating his own party, Option nationale, in 2011. In 2013, he left Quebec to work with an investment firm in Britain, returning to rejoin the Parti Québécois as a candidate in the 2018 election.—Trans.

12 Pierre Karl Péladeau was member of the national assembly for Saint-Jérôme riding from 2014 to 2016 and leader of the Parti Québécois from 2015 to 2016. Owner of Québecor, the media and telecommunications company founded by his father, he spearheaded the company's aggressive expansion. As party leader, he courted controversy in relation to anti-union positions and comments in 2015 suggesting that Quebec might enter negotiations with First Nations regarding territorial borders in the event of its separation from Canada.—Trans.

13 Bernard Drainville was a Parti Québécois member of the national assembly from 2007 to 2016, serving under the Pauline Marois government as minister responsible for democratic institutions and active citizenship. In that position, in 2013, not long before a provincial election, he introduced the controversial Quebec Charter of Values, or Bill 60, which, in its interpretation of the "reasonable accommodation" of ethno-cultural and religious minority groups, proposed an official secularism prohibiting public sector employees from wearing or displaying religious symbols, implicitly targeting non-Christian groups. Later legislation, passed under the Coalition Avenir Québec government in 2019, Bill 21 or the Act respecting the laicity of the State, maintains the principles and coded discrimination of this earlier Charter.—Trans.

14 *Ti-pop* refers to a Pop Art–influenced artistic and political current of the 1960s in Quebec that rejected the search for Québécois authenticity in traditional folklore, turning instead to a validation of the kitsch aesthetics of popular consumer culture. Catherine Fournier, elected mayor of Longueil in 2021, was the youngest member of the National Assembly of Quebec from 2017 until 2019. She quit the PQ in 2019 to sit as an independent, pledging to forge a new independence movement.—Trans.

15 Giroux distinguishes between the *mouvement indépendantiste* begun in the 1950s and the sovereigntism that emerged in the late 1960s. The goals of the former were broader than sovereignty.—Trans.

16 Denise Bombardier is a journalist and essayist, especially prominent on Radio-Canada television in the 1980s. She holds a doctoral degree in sociology from the Sorbonne and is noted for her use of a European-normed French. —Trans.

17 "Third link" or *le troisième lien*, refers to a long-promised, grand construction project, a tunnel that would connect the city of Lévis, on the south shore of the Saint Lawrence Seaway, to Quebec City.—Trans.

18 In the line from the song written in 1975 by poet Gilles Vigneault, "*Les Gens du pays*" (also sometimes called "*L'hymne du Québec*"), the words are prefaced by an address to the people, hence, "People of my country, it is your turn to let yourselves speak of love." The song is regularly sung on Saint-Jean-Baptiste Day, June 24, an official national holiday in Quebec.—Trans.

19 With the expression "Québec Inc.," Giroux refers to Québécois entrepreneurialism in the last forty years and its resulting inequalities.—Trans.

CHAPTER FOUR

1 [Translation] Jacques Ferron, *Historiettes* (Montreal: Éditions due jour, 1969), 48.

2 Giroux uses *parole* in the original, drawing on a distinction in structural linguistics between language approached as an abstract system of rules (*langue*) and language as it is spoken or written by actual speakers in concrete situations, in utterances that bear the marks of socio-historical context or individual (or collective) creativity (*parole*).—Trans.

3 *Joual* is a name for the non-standard, spoken version of a popular French, mixed with English, that emerged in Quebec in the context of industrialization

in the nineteenth century. While it has been used as a denigrating term for the French spoken by working-class or regional speakers, *joual* also has been reclaimed as an integral aspect of Québécois identity. Giroux's approach, however, as Marie-Hélène Constant has pointed out, is not identitarian; rather, she is interested in the decolonial and hybridizing energies of the French vernaculars of North America. See Marie-Hélène Constant, "Investir ailleurs: Compte rendu de *Parler en Amérique. Oralité, colonialisme, térritoire* de Dalie Giroux," *Spirale* 271 (2020): 82–5.—Trans.

4 On the epistemology of this approach, see Dalie Giroux, "L'espace et le temps de l'émancipation: Essai sur le parole," *Canadian Journal of Political Science/Revue Canadienne de science politique* 41, no. 3 (2008): 49–67.

5 A method of literary montage, the dialectical image was developed by Walter Benjamin (1892–1940), the German Jewish Marxist philosopher of history, in his *Arcades Project* (1927–1940). It involves the juxtaposition of images of "then" and "now" in such a way as to disrupt the view of history as tradition or progress, bringing the interruptive force of discarded details into the present. A tension between codes exposes the transitory, ideological, or phantasmatic, in a way that points to what may be dangerous in the present.—Trans.

6 On the culture of pow-wows in northeastern America, see Dalie Giroux, "La culture contemporaine du pow-wow chez les nations autochtones de l'est Canadien: Figures et movement de la renaissance indigène en Amérique du Nord," *Géographie et cultures* 96 (2015): 85–108.

7 The heading appears in English in the original.—Trans.

8 Georges Dor (1931–2001), a Québécois singer, songwriter, journalist, playwright, and producer, released his first album, which included the massively popular "La Manic," in 1966. The lyrics take the form of a love letter written by a lonely construction worker on a dam-building site ("Manic," on the falls of the Manicouagan River). Dor began his working life in a factory and then on a dam site; he is seen as a national *chansonnier* who created myths from everyday life.—Trans.

9 Innu writer and political activist An Antane Kapesh (1926–2004) was band chief at Schefferville (the Matimekush reserve) in the Côte-Nord region of Quebec in 1965 to 1966. Her 1976 autobiography, providing an account of dispossession, displacement, and residential schooling, *Je suis une maudit sauvagesse/Eukuan nin matshimanitu innu-iskueu*, was published in a French-Innu edition in 1976 and in a revised edition in 2019. Her 1979 book *Tante*

nana etutamin mitassi?/Qu'as-tu fait de mon pays?, also adapted for the stage, recounts the colonization of Turtle Island through the experience of a child. —Trans.

10 An Antane Kapesh, *Eukuan nin matshi-manitu innushkueu/I Am a Damn Savage, Tanite nene etutamin nitassi?/What Have You Done to My Country?*, trans. Sarah Henzi (Waterloo: Wilfrid Laurier University Press, 2020 [1976 and 1979]), 139.

11 Pierre Perrault (1927–1999), a Québécois documentary filmmaker celebrated for his contributions to the direct documentary style of the 1960s, is credited with having developed a "cinema of speech" or "living cinema" through his representations of the lifeways of rural, working-class Québécois. *Pour la suite du monde* (1963), the first film in his Île-aux-Coudres triology, is a portrait of the lives of beluga whale hunters living on this island in the Saint Lawrence River. The first Quebec (and Canadian) film to be screened at the Cannes Film Festival, the documentary deploys the techniques of direct cinema, which include hand-held cameras and the omission of voice-over narration.—Trans.

12 For "lack of genius," Giroux references a French Canadian expression, naming it as such: "*comme on dit en language canadienne parlée, si on extrapole, un 'sans genie.*'"—Trans.

13 Daniel Francis, *The Imaginary Indian* (Vancouver: Arsenal Pulp, 2004), 145.

14 The influence of the Boy Scouts in Quebec is notable given that the tie to the British Empire through a sense of imperial Canadian identity was central to the spread of Scouting in Canada. The Boy Scouts Association of Canada, initially led by men with military connections, was established as a branch of the Boy Scouts Association of the United Kingdom and then incorporated as a Canadian association in 1914. See Patricia Dirks, "Canada's Boys – An Imperial or National Asset? Responses to Baden-Powell's Boy Scout Movement in Pre-War Canada," *Canada and the British World: Culture, Migration, and Identity*, edited by Phillip Buckner and R. Douglas Francis (Vancouver: University of British Columbia Press, 2006), 113, 114.—Trans.

15 Giroux refers to the 1967 book by French author Guy Debord, *The Society of the Spectacle*, which develops the thesis that in capitalist modernity, everyday practices, social relations, even physical infrastructure are constituted through the circularity of representation, via the consumption of reified perceptions and experiences.—Trans.

16 A decade-long revival would follow, with a final closure in 1998 when the

county assumed control of the property due to unpaid taxes. The economy of
northern New York State, Vermont, and Maine (much like that of Quebec's
borderland) had rested on forestry and mining, from the era of colonization
on. The decline of these industries in the early twentieth century opened the
way for a tourist economy based on fishing and hunting. The history of the
land on which Frontier Town was built is typical of the British colonial frontier in North America. Abenaki and Mohawk territory, surveyed and priva-
tized in the nineteenth century, passed from the hands of the poor farmer
who bought it in 1916 into the hands of a tourism promoter in the 1950s, who
founded Frontier Town. The property title transferred in 1916 was appropriated for the building of a railway that was to go to an iron ore mine. The railway never saw the light of day. For almost fifty years, economic activity in the
region was concentrated in Frontier Town. Today the site is in ruin and is
slated for various public-private tourism development projects. For a detailed
study of Indigenous presence in the Adirondacks, including the relations
between this Indigenous presence and tourism, see Melissa Otis, "At Home in
the Adirondacks: A Regional History of Indigenous and Euroamerican Inter-
actions, 1776–1920" (doctoral thesis, University of Toronto, 2013).

17 On this aesthetic, see Dalie Giroux, "Colonial Kitsch," in *Entrepreneurs du
commun: Monument aux victimes de la liberté* (Gatineau: UQO Gallery, 2015).

18 Giroux offers "*savoir vaseux*" as a paraphrase for Michael Taussig's "epistemic
murk" here. She uses the Foucauldian distinction between *savoir* and *connaissance* to draw on the difference between knowledge as received and crystallized into a discipline (*connaissance*) and knowledge as the less explicit
conditions for knowing in a certain time and place (*savoir*). Importantly, for
Foucault, it is in relation to *savoir* that it is possible to practice detachment
and disidentification. On what she calls the "*savoir vaseux de la frontière*," see
Giroux's "L'espace de mort et la mémoire de la liberté," in *Généalogie du
déracinement: Enquête sur l'habitation postcoloniale.*—Trans.

19 Swift Eagle grew up in the Santo Domingo Pueblo community in New Mexico, speaking Keresan, the language of the Keres Pueblo. He attended the Santa
Fe Indian Boarding School. Raising his children with his wife, Chee Chee Bird,
of the Chickahominy tribe, he taught Indigenous arts, modelled, and performed for a living in Frontier Town, determined to "teach his children the
traditional skills the Indian school had worked so hard to erase in him." Debo-

rah Medenbach, "Sharing and Restoring the Heritage of American Indians," *Times Herald Record Online*, 21 March 2007. https://www.recordonline.com/article/20070321/COMM/703210302.—Trans.

20 https://projectabsurd.wordpress.com/2009/09/10/frontier-town-north-hudson-ny. Post published in 2011.

21 An Antane Kapesh, *Eukuan nin matshi-manitu innushkueu/I Am a Damn Savage*, 35.

22 Gail Valaskakis, "Postcards of My Past," *Indian Country: Essays on Contemporary Native Culture* (Waterloo: Wilfrid Laurier University Press, 2005), 76–7.

23 Gerald Vizenor, *Manifest Manners: Narratives on Postindian Survivance* (Lincoln and London: University of Nebraska Press, 1999), vii.

24 Joachim Guillaume Lamothe (1920–1992), born in Saint-Hyacinthe, Quebec, was an actor and French-language country music star who recorded over 500 songs.—Trans.

25 Hector de Saint-Denys Garneau, "C'est eux qui m'ont tué," trans. John Glassco, *Complete Poems of Saint Denys Garneau* (Oberon Press, 1975 [1949]), 160.

26 Rémi Savard, *Destins d'Amérique: Les Autochtones et nous* (Montreal: L'Hexagone, 1979), 156.

CHAPTER FIVE

1 Robert Hébert, *Novation: Philosophie artisanale* (Montreal: Liver, 2004), 150.

2 Georges E. Sioui is a Wendat historian, philosopher, poet, songwriter, and professor at the University of Ottawa. Born in Wendake, Quebec, in 1948, he is a member of the Tseawi (Rising Sun) clan. He received his PhD in history from Laval University in 1991 and has worked in Indigenous health, cultural preservation, and education projects. In 1990, Sioui, along with his four brothers, won a landmark legal victory over territorial and traditional land use rights at the Supreme Court of Canada.—Trans.

3 This renaissance is strongly connected to Red Power in the United States, the movement through which Indigenous youth, influenced by the civil rights movement, called for the self-determination of Indigenous people in America. More powerfully, though, the resurgence was inspired and nourished by an Indigenous literary, academic, and artistic movement. In Canada, the catalyst

for this resurgence movement is seen to be the Indigenous opposition to the 1969 White Paper proposed by Jean Chrétien and Pierre Trudeau, which proposed, among other things, the abolition of the Indian Act.

4 The 2007 UNDRIP was officially recognized in Canada only in 2021, when Parliament passed the United Declaration on the Rights of Indigenous Peoples Act. The House of Commons Apology to Inuit, Métis, and First Nations Peoples for Residential Schools was made 2008. The TRC gathered testimony from survivors of the Indian Residential School system from 2010 to 2014 and issued its Final Report in 2015. The National Inquiry into Missing and Murdered Indigenous Women and Girls (2016–19) involved a truth gathering process and the publication of a Final Report. The Viens Commission (or Public Inquiry Commission on relations between Indigenous Peoples and certain public services in Quebec) was launched in response to media exposures of Indigenous women's disappearances and their allegations of police abuse in the Abitibi region.—Trans.

5 In the winter of 2020, when the hereditary Wet'suwet'en chiefs in northern British Columbia and their supporters who were blocking the road to a Coastal GasLink drill site were served an injunction by the RCMP, solidarity blockades took place in ports and on rail lines and bridges in other Indigenous communities and urban centres in BC, Manitoba, Ontario, Nova Scotia, and Quebec.—Trans.

6 Giroux provides the titles of the original French editions: *Pour une histoire autochtone de l'Amérique* and *Les Hurons-Wendat: Une civilization méconnue*. The English translations were published in 1992 and 1999, respectively.—Trans.

7 Georges E. Sioui, *Histoires de Kanatha: Essais et discours, 1991–2008/Histories of Kanatha: Essays and Discourses, 1991–2008*, selected and introduced by Dalie Giroux (Ottawa: University of Ottawa Press, 2009). Sioui's essays and speeches are published either in French or English in this collection, depending on the language in which they first appeared or were delivered.—Trans.

8 *Habitus* is the term used by French sociologist Pierre Bourdieu for the embodied experience of structured social relations, insofar as those relations are lived as schemes of taste, styles of thought and discourse, gesture, and action. An ensemble of dispositions developed through a group's (sometimes a generation's) navigation of different social settings, *habitus* is both deeply engrained and subject to shifts across space and time. See Pierre Bourdieu, *The Logic of Practice* (Stanford: Stanford University Press, 1980).—Trans.

9   Vine Deloria Jr. (1933–2005) was a Standing Rock Sioux philosopher and ac-
    tivist, and a professor of history, law, political science, and religious studies.
    His critique of Western science is developed in *Red Earth, White Lies: Native
    Americans and the Myth of Scientific Fact* (1995).—Trans.

10 Giroux's *parole* is here translated as "thought."—Trans.

11 The word "*âme*" in the original has been translated as *habitus* here.

12 The approach I propose does not engage in denunciation of those who are
    "colonial," nor in drawing sharp distinctions between those who are and those
    who are not so (especially not in an individualizing register). I believe that
    dealing with the psychic, intimate matter of colonialism requires some care
    not to inflame the kinds of dynamics that create scapegoats, stigmas, and bi-
    nary oppositions between the good and the bad. This care is in order to avoid
    feeding the beast as opposed to combatting it, and multiplying blind spots. On
    the ethical and political questions related to the specularity of colonial repre-
    sentations, see Thierry Hentsch, *L'Orient imaginaire: La vision politique occi-
    dentale de l'Est meditérraneen* (Paris: Minuit, 1988) and Dalie Giroux, "Thierry
    Hentsch/Proche-Orient: Désarticulation amoureuse de la puissance du
    négatif," *Cahiers de l'idiotie* 2 (2009): 221–66.

13 Gaston Miron, "Séquences," *L'homme rapaillé* (Montreal: Typo, 1996 [1970]),
    76. Giroux cites the original line, "*batèche de mon grand-père dans le noire
    analphabète.*" In the 1950s, Miron (1928–1996), a passionate sovereigntist and
    key figure in the literary and cultural activity connected to the Quiet Revolu-
    tion, founded Hexagone, the first Québécois publishing house dedicated to
    poetry. A partial translation of *L'homme rapaillé*, one of the central texts in
    modern Quebec literature, was published as *The March to Love: Selected Poems*
    (n.p.: International Poetry forum/Byblos Edition, 1986), but does not include
    "Séquences."—Trans.

14 "Keb" is a slang term – in linguistic terms, an apocope, in which sounds or
    letters at the end of a word are dropped to make a new word – used to refer
    mockingly to those who consider themselves authentically Québécois, or to
    the culture celebrated as such. The term can signal strong disidentification
    from the Keb as other or simply mild self-mockery.—Trans.

15 On the question of settler envy of the colonized in the context of Quebec, see
    Geneviève Page, "'Est-ce qu'on peut etre racisées, nous aussi?': Les féministes
    blanches et le désir de racisation," in Naima Hamrouni and Chantal Maillé,
    Le sujet du féminisme est-il blanc? Femmes racisées et recherche féministe

(Montreal: Les éditions du remue-ménage, 2015), 133–54; Darryl Leroux, *Distorted Descent: White Claims to Indigenous Identity* (Winnipeg: University of Manitoba Press, 2019).

16 [Translation] Yvon Rivard, "L'héritage de la pauvreté," *Littérature* 17 (1998): 211. Rivard is interpreting a philosophical meditation in the journal of Saint-Denys Garneau from 1939, entitled "Le mauvais pauvre va parmi vous avec son regard en dessous." See Hector Saint-Denys Garneau, *Saint-Denys Garneau: Textes choisis et présentés par Benoit Lacroix* (Montreal and Paris: Fides, 1956), 84–8.—Trans.

17 From here on, "*mauvais pauvre*" is translated as "pauper."—Trans.

18 [Translation] Saint-Denys Garneau, *Saint-Denys Garneau.*

19 [Translation] Georges E. Sioui, "La signification interculturelle de l'Américité: Point de vue Wendat sur les transferts culturels Europe-Amérique, 1992–1992," in *Histoires de Kanatha*, 46–7.

20 Ibid.

21 Pierrot-Ross Tremblay, *Thou Shalt Forget: Indigenous Sovereignty, Resistance and the Production of Cultural Oblivion in Canada* (London: University of London Press, 2019), 58.

22 [Translation] Rosa Pires, *Ne sommes-nous pas Québécoises?*, 93.

23 Wendake is made up of two urban reserves of the Huron-Wendat Nation and surrounded by the Quebec City borough of La Haute-Saint-Charles. The traditional territory of the Wendat, who formed part of the Wyandot Confederacy, stretches from the Saint Lawrence River valley to the Great Lakes region. When war and disease dispersed the Wyandot Confederacy in the seventeenth century, the Wendat resettled in what was then called the village of Lorette. —Trans.

24 The texts of these presentations, as well as those of a roundtable entitled "Nomos de L'Amérique en question," were published independently in 2007, as the first six issues of the now-defunct journal *Cahiers de l'idiotie.*

25 On Pocahontas and the figure of the Indigenous woman in the colonial imaginary, see Gail Valaskakis, "Postcards of My Past," *Indian Country: Essays on Contemporary Native Culture* (Waterloo: Wilfrid Laurier University Press, 2005), 125–50.

26 The 1990 "Oka Crisis," also called the Oka resistance or the Kanesatake resistance, involved a response by the Québécois police, RCMP, and Canadian army to Mohawk protestors at the Kanesatake reserve north of Montreal who were

attempting to stop the expansion of a nearby golf course and housing development into adjacent disputed territory. The events are significant for the militarized response as well as the mobilization and involvement of Indigenous allies from across the country, including protestors from the nearby Mohawk community of Kahnawake who blockaded the Mercier bridge to Montreal in support of Kanesatake.—Trans.

27 Sioui, "La signification interculturelle de l'Américité," 35.

28 John Borrows, "Earth-Bound: Indigenous Law and Environmental Reconciliation," in *Resurgence and Reconciliation: Indigenous-Settler Relations and Earth Teachings*, eds. Michael Asch, John Borrows, and James Tully (Toronto: University of Toronto Press, 2018), 69.

29 [Translation] Radio-Canada, "Les Atikamekw déclarent leur souveraineté," 8 September 2014. https://ici.radio-canada.ca/nouvelle/683598/nation-atikamekw-declaration-souverainete-territoire.

30 Aaron Mills, "Rooted Constitutionalism: Growing Political Community," in *Resurgence and Reconciliation: Indigenous-Settler Relations and Earth Teachings*, eds. Michael Asch, John Borrows and James Tully (Toronto: University of Toronto Press, 2018), 135.

31 [Translation] Georges E. Sioui, personal communication with the author. The work Sioui mentions in the quotation is his *Eatenonha: Native Roots of Modern Democracy* (Montreal and Kingston: McGill-Queen's University Press, 2019).

32 Rémi Savard, cited in Georges E. Sioui, *For an Amerindian Autohistory: An Essay on the Foundations of a Social Ethic*, trans. Sheila Fischman (Montreal and Kingston: McGill-Queen's University Press, 1992), 23; Rémi Savard, *Destins d'Amerique: les autochtones et nous* (Montreal: Hexagone, 1979), 15.

CHAPTER SIX

1 Robert Hébert, *Rudiments d'us* (Trois-Rivières: Écrits des Forges, 1979), 46.

2 Quebec writer Pierre Morency has won Governor General's Awards in the categories of French fiction and non-fiction and in 2000 won the Prix Athanase-David for his body of work.—Trans.

3 Poitevin, a person from the Poitou region of France, also the name of the dialect spoken in this western region. Note that later in the chapter, Giroux makes the parenthetical observation that Poitou was the birthplace of Michel Foucault.—Trans.

4 The Royal 22nd Regiment is an infantry regiment of the Canadian Army founded in 1914 and known as "*le Vingt-deuxième*." A largely francophone regiment, as its recruits are drawn from Quebec, its headquarters are in the Citadel of Quebec. The regiment was involved in combat in Europe during the First and Second World Wars and was the source of the troops present during the so-called Oka Crisis in 1990 at Kanesatake.—Trans.

5 [Translation] Pierre Morency, *A l'heure du loup* (Montreal: Boréal, 2002), 113–14.

6 Jean Giono (1895–1970) was a French novelist whose early novels were peopled by peasants and infused with a pantheistic view of nature.—Trans.

7 For a very precise portrait of the cruelty in farm life and the related family power relations, see the powerful short story collection by Geneviève Boudreau, *La vie au-dehors* (Montreal: Boréal, 2019). Two stories in particular, concerning cattle, crystallize my point: "Pas la peine," and "La clé de la Barbe bleue."

8 [Translation] Jos-Phydime Michaud, *Kamouraska de mémoire... Souvenirs de la vie d'un village Québécois recueillis par Fernand Archambault* (Paris: François-Maspéro, 1981), 102.

9 *Avoir l'oeil, avoir à l'oeil, tenir à l'oeil.*—Trans.

10 [Translation] Marc Fumaroli, *Le livre des métaphores: Essay sur la mémoire de la langue française* (Paris: Robert Laffont, 2012), 132.

11 Paul Virilio, *Speed and Politics*, trans. Mark Polizzotti (Los Angeles: Semiotext(e), 2006), 94.

12 The ancient Greek *nomos* means both the official rules and the cultural habits sustaining a group's social and political life. It is used by the German political theorist Carl Schmitt in his 1950 work, *Nomos of the Earth*.—Trans.

13 Jean de La Fontaine (1621–1695) was a French writer whose twelve books of *Fables*, published between 1668 and 1694, retold in verse form fables derived from ancient as well as contemporary sources. The *Fables* generated a number of standard and proverbial phrases in the French language.—Trans.

14 Jean de La Fontaine, *The Fables of La Fontaine*, trans. R. Thomson (London: J. C. Nimmo and Bain, 1884), 98. Giroux uses the two-volume translation by Marc Fumaroli, *La Fontaine: Fables* (Paris: Imprimerie nationale, 1985).

15 Giroux references Gertrude Stein's *The Geographical History of America* (Baltimore and London: Johns Hopkins University Press, 1995 [1936]), 49. In that text, Stein's narrator appreciates the abstract lines and geometrical space of

America from the point of view of a spare, modernist aesthetic. Notably, in the 1930s, Stein was critical of the Roosevelt administration's moves to complicate this nation-statist space through recognition of tribal sovereignty. See Aaron Nyerges, "Styling Sovereignty: Gertrude Stein's Epideictic Constitution of the USA," *Textual Practice* 31, no. 1 (2017): 59–79. Giroux's quotation associates the statement by Stein's narrator with the point of view of the master. —Trans.

16 René Guénon (1886–1951) was a prolific French writer whose varied works critiqued modern European civilization and sought to establish a "Primordial Tradition" on the basis of recurrent ideas in religious doctrines and esotericisms, including Catholic Christianity, Islam, Sufism, Hinduism, the Kabbalah, Vedanta, as well as folklore and mythology.—Trans.

17 Réné Guénon, *Fundamental Symbols: The Universal Language of Sacred Science*, trans. Alvin Moore Jr. (Bartlow, Cambridge: Quinta Essentia, 1995), 295.

18 Jean de La Fontaine, *The Fables of La Fontaine*.

19 [Translation] Marc Fumaroli, *La Fontaine: Fables*, vol. 1, bks. 1–4 (Paris: Imprimerie nationale, 1985), 383. Fumaroli interprets the lines that La Fontaine takes from Phaedrus as suggesting a "retrospective, allegorical reading of this account of life on the farm" in which the lover could correspond to each of the identities listed. La Fontaine thereby conjoins the so-called "moral" of the fable with a "hermeneutic lesson. The fables are written in the 'language of the gods' which hides as much at it reveals, and does not open itself to the lazy reader. The eye of the master, the eye of the lover, these are also the eye of the real reader." Fumaroli, 383.—Trans.

20 Pertinent in this regard are the recent archaeological discoveries demonstrating that agriculture and the state are not necessary companions – the practices for domesticating plants and animals appearing thousands of years before the state form and being conducted without it long after its historical appearances and disappearances. In this sense, the state is not the necessarily corollary of agriculture, and this form of society, the modern colonial form, is not a "natural" stage in the evolution of humanity. See James C. Scott, *Against the Grain: A Deep History of the Earliest States* (New Haven, CT: Yale University Press, 2017).

21 Samuel de Champlain, *The Works of Samuel de Champlain, Volume II, 1608–1613*, book 2, chapter 5, trans. John Squair (Toronto: Champlain Society, 1925), 52.

22 Ibid., chapter 4, 37.

23 Ibid., chapter 4, 44.

24 Yves Chrétien, Denys Delâge, and Sylvie Vincent, *Au croisement de nos destins: Quand Ueipishtikueiau devint Québec* (Montreal: Recherches amérindiennes au Québec, 2009).

25 Champlain, *Works of Samuel de Champlain*, 1–51.

26 Yves Chrétien, Denys Delâge, and Sylvie Vincent, *Au croisement de nos destins*, 65.

27 See for example, Northrop Frye's famous figure for "the way in which the Canadian imagination has developed in its literature" the "garrison mentality," which he saw as arising from the experience of the small settler community turned in upon itself in order to defend against a perceived threatening otherness. Frye's discussion is both unreflectively Eurocentric in the totalizing implications of its claims and, at the same time, specific about the British-originating settler psyche and political culture he is describing. Northrop Frye, "Conclusion to *A Literary History of Canada*" [1965/1971], in *Unhomely States: Theorizing English-Canadian Postcolonialism*, ed. Cynthia Sugars (Peterborough, ON: Broadview Press, 2004), 14.—Trans.

28 Already unmasked by Jacques Ferron in the 1960s (see his *Historiettes*, 135 ff), this construct is also put into question by Georges E. Sioui in the chapter entitled "The Destruction of Huronia" in his *For an Amerindian Autohistory* (Montreal and Kingston: McGill-Queen's University Press, 1992), 23.

29 Stefano Harney and Fred Moten, *The Undercommons: Fugitive Planning and Black Study* (Wivenhoe, NY: Minor Compositions, 2013), 17.

30 Ibid.

31 From 1871 and 1921, following the transfer of lands in the West from the Hudson's Bay Company to Canada, eleven Numbered Treaties were signed between First Nations and the Crown. Although the details of the negotiations and treaty terms varied somewhat, there was an overriding discrepancy between the First Nations' understandings and incentives – to formalize relationship and land-sharing through diplomatic agreement, to transition to agriculture in the context of dwindling bison herds, to access protections from European diseases – and those of the Canadian government, which intended, rather, to control the movement of Indigenous peoples and free up land for colonial settlement and industrial development.—Trans.

32 [Translation] Naomi Fontaine, *Shuni: Ce que tu dois savoir, Julie* (Montreal: Mémoire d'encrier, 2019), 16.

33 Recall the story of Marie-Josephte Corriveau, "La Corriveau," hanged and exposed in an iron cage on Saint-Joseph Street at Pointe-Lévy by a British military court in 1763. The misogynist legend has long haunted childhoods along the south shore of the Saint Lawrence.

34 [Translation] Fontaine, *Naomi Fontaine*, 16–17.

35 *"Incyste"* is Simon Labrecque's term, discussed in his "Remarques sur le concept d'incystence: Un cas d'auto-traduction," *Trahir*, 14 May 2014. https://trahir.wordpress.com/2014/05/14/labrecque-incystence. [In this essay, Labrecque notes that he wishes to draw on the English "cyst," in addition to ancient Greek and Latin etymologies, which together carry the sense of an insistent, though buried, phenomenon.—Trans.

36 [Translation] Fontaine, *Shuni*, 19.

37 Pierrot Ross-Tremblay, "L'oubli n'est pas absolu: Réminiscences et prise de parole chez les Premiers peuples de la francophonie des Amériques," in *Minorités linguistiques et société/Linguistic Minorities and Society* 4 (2014): 215.

CONCLUSION

1 [Translation] Frédérique Bernier, *Hantises: Carnets de Frida Burns sur quelques morceaux de vie et de littérature* (Montreal: Nota bene, 2020), 36.

2 Giroux uses the expression coined by Giles Deleuze and Felix Guattari in their *Kafka: Toward a Minor Literature* (1986) in order to theorize literatures issuing from subaltern spaces, rejecting the aspiration to become central, and seeking instead to hold open the space for new connections. Giroux writes about Deleuze's reading of Kafka in "Tentation d'évasion hors de la sphere paternelle: Lecture et anarchie chez Gilles Deleuze," in *Contr'hommage pour Gilles Deleuze: nouvelles lectures, nouvelles écritures*, ed. Dalie Giroux et al. (Quebec City: University of Laval Press, 2009).—Trans.

3 "The Metaphor of the Accident: A New Historical Paradigm for the Inclusion of Canada's First Peoples," in Georges E. Sioui, *Histoires de Kanatha: Essais et discours, 1991–2008/Histories of Kanatha: Essays and Discourses, 1991–2008*, selected and introduced by Dalie Giroux (Ottawa: University of Ottawa Press, 2009), 309–13.

4 [Translation] Julia Posca, *Le manifeste des parvenus: Le* think big *des pense-petit* (Montreal: Lux Éditeur, 2018), 34.

5 [Translation] Mathieu Bélisle, *Bienvenue au pays de la vie ordinaire* (Montreal: Leméac, 2017), 13.

6 Malcom Ferdinand, *A Decolonial Ecology: Thinking from the Caribbean World*, trans. Anthony Paul Smith (Polity, 2022).

7 [Translation] Declaration of the Atikamekw and Montagnais Council to the Quebec premier, René Lévesque, on the occasion of the meeting at Quebec City on 14 September 1978. Printed in *Le Devoir*, 20 December 1978, 5.

8 [Translation] Yves-Marie Abraham, *Guérir du mal de l'infini: Produire moins, partager plus, décider ensemble* (Montreal: Ecosociété, 2019), 232–3.

9 Corinne Larochelle, *Vent debout* (Montreal: Editions du Noroit, 2007), 64.

10 Réjean Ducharme (1941–2017) was a Québécois novelist known for his reclusive existence and his dense linguistic style, established in his first published novel, *L'Avalée des avalés*, which provides a child protagonist's furious rejection of the adult world through interior monologue. Published in Paris in 1966, when Ducharme was just twenty-four, the novel was shortlisted for the Prix Goncourt, and granted the Governor General's Award for French-language fiction. It is seen as a foundational text for modern Quebec literature. English translations appeared in 1968 (*The Swallower Swallowed*) and 2000 (*Swallowed*).—Trans.

11 Réjean Ducharme, *The Daughter of Christopher Columbus*, trans. Will Browning (Montreal: Guernica, 2000 [1969]), 124.

12 [Translation] Gilles McMillan, *La contamination des mots* (Montreal: Lux Éditeur, 2014), 262.